Let Us Keep the Feast

Food from the Foothills of South Carolina
Church of the Redeemer Episcopal

The cookbook is a collection of favorite recipes,
which are not necessarily original recipes.

Let Us Keep the Feast
Food from the Foothills of South Carolina

Copyright© 2002
Church of the Redeemer Episcopal
120 Mauldin Road
Greenville, South Carolina 29605
864-277-4562

LC Control Number: 2001 135517
ISBN: 0-9712715-0-X

Edited, Designed, and Manufactured by Favorite Recipes® Press
an imprint of

FRP™

P.O. Box 305142
Nashville, Tennessee 37230
800-358-0560

Book Design: Brad Whitfield, Susan Breining
Art Director: Steve Newman
Project Manager: Ginger Dawson

Manufactured in the United States of America
First Printing: 2002
5,000 copies

Cookbook Committee

Church of the Redeemer

Doris Gant
Kirsten Hansen
Talle Hiltabidle
Bill Lee
Patti Lee
Betty Lupo
Lauren McCullough
Janice Peele
Kelley Roseberry
Kathy Shugart
Elise Watson
Kellie Wilson
Caroline Witbeck
Mary Ann Wood

Church of the Redeemer
50 Years of Serving God

The 2001 stewardship drive has faithfully begun,
At the Church of the Redeemer, born in 1951.
Happy Birthday Redeemer—Now 50 years old.
The people and ministries here, are worth more than gold.

More than a building, more than land
A history of people who prayed and planned.
To have a place of worship, where God's work was done.
Not any different than us in 2001.

Our desires are many, our goal is one,
To continue all the work that God had begun.
To spread His good word to all that we know,
To help those in need, to help them to grow.

Offer up your loving pledges at this time we pray,
Your time and talents are needed each and every day.
When the future Redeemer family reflects, on all we have done,
They too will know we spread God's word like those in '51.

—Kathy Shugart

Contents

Church of the Redeemer
1951-2001

On the evening of March 1, 1951, a meeting was held in the auditorium of Augusta Circle School to look into the possibility of establishing an Episcopal Parish in the Augusta Road area of Greenville. The final organizational meeting was held on April 23, 1951. Although there was no budget in 1951, the group agreed on a tentative budget of $9,000 for the year 1952.

The name Church of the Redeemer was chosen for the new parish. The Rev. John T. Harrison was called as Redeemer's first rector. The first service at the Church of the Redeemer was held at the Buckhorn Fishing Camp at Paris Mountain State Park on Sunday, June 3, 1951. Bishop Gravatt celebrated Holy Eucharist. A picnic lunch was served to the eighty-seven people in attendance.

After worship services were held in the cafeteria at Augusta Circle School for several months, ground was broken on July 7, 1952, for a new church building, the first Episcopal church to be built in Greenville in more than forty years. On September 7, 1952, the first worship service was held in the new building that has since been named Purser Hall in honor of The Rev. J. Philip Purser who served as rector from 1981 to 2000.

The current church building was completed in 1958 but was gutted by fire in 1969. Extensive repairs were completed and the church reopened in 1970. Another complete renovation of the sanctuary, nave, and narthex was completed in 1991, giving Redeemer one of the most beautiful sanctuaries in Greenville.

The Church of the Redeemer staff includes a full-time rector and assistant rector, deacon, organist/choir director, bookkeeper, nursery director, director of education, director of young adult ministries, church secretary, and a sexton.

Redeemer provides numerous educational programs for both adults and youth, consisting of two Godly Play classes, one for preschoolers and another for first and second graders, and a Sanctus Workshop for grades three to five.

Journey to Adulthood is a program Redeemer offers to prepare youth for confirmation and involvement in the life in the church. It consists of Rite 13 for grades six and seven, J2A for grades eight and nine, and YAC for grades ten to twelve.

A Vacation Bible School program is offered each summer.

Adult classes include TNT (Twenties 'N Thirties) for young adults, Adult Forum, Pilgrims in Christ, three Bible study classes, and the Coffee Class, which provides an opportunity for lively, open discussion and fellowship. There are also programs for adults and children during special seasons such as Lent and Advent.

Fellowship and service opportunities for men and women are also provided by the Episcopal Church Women (ECW), three women's guilds, and a men's group.

Outreach programs supported by Redeemer include the Pleasant Valley Commons, Project Host Soup Kitchen, United Ministries Food Bank, Shepherd's Gate, York Place Children's Home, Miracle Hill Children's Home, World Missions in Haiti, and the Annual Angel Wreath Gift Program.

Redeemer's mission statement sums up the values its parishioners hold most dear: A community celebrating, sharing and serving Christ, the Redeemer.

The Redeemer church family is proud of its reputation as one of the friendliest and most diverse congregations in the Greenville area. Redeemer is currently the church home to over 350 people.

Rectors Serving Church of the Redeemer

The Rev. John T. Harrison, 1952–1955

The Rev. Grant O. Folmsbee, 1956–1961

The Rev. Clyde L. Ireland, 1961–1970

The Rev. Edsel L. Keith, 1971–1978

The Rev. Ralph S. Dean, 1979–1980

The Rev. J. Philip Purser, 1981–2000

Appetizers & Beverages

Belgian Endive Crudités   10

Sweet Ginger Melon Balls   10

Four-Cheese Puffs   11

Chinese Sausage Bites   11

Cheddar-Stuffed Mushrooms   12

Seafood-Stuffed Mushrooms   12

Wild Mushroom Tarts   13

Crispy Cheese Straws   14

Ice Box Cheese Wafers   14

Vegetable Squares   15

Cajun Snacks   15

Artichoke and Jack Dip with
  Pita Chips   16

Carolina Caviar   17

Caviar Pie   17

Hummus   18

Layered Taco Dip   18

Vidalia Onion Dip   19

Warm Herb Cheese Spread   19

Cream Cheese Ball   20

Smoked Salmon Ball   20

Orange Julius   21

Eggnog   21

Hot Buttered Rum   22

Irish Cream   22

Fruit Smoothie   23

Hot Mulled Punch   23

Belgian Endive Crudités

1 head Belgian endive, leaves
    separated
1 tablespoon sour cream
1 tablespoon cream cheese
Juice of 1/4 lemon
Salt to taste

White pepper to taste
Cayenne pepper to taste
Smoked salmon slices
Capers (optional)
Chopped fresh dill

    Rinse the endive leaves and pat dry. Combine the sour cream, cream cheese, lemon juice, salt, white pepper and cayenne pepper in a small bowl and mix until smooth. Spoon a small amount onto the base of each endive leaf. Place a small salmon slice on top of each leaf. Top with the capers and sprinkle with the dill. Arrange on a serving plate and serve immediately. You may also prepare using steamed artichoke leaves in place of the endive.
    Yield: 8 servings

Sweet Ginger Melon Balls

1 cantaloupe, seeded
1 honeydew melon, seeded

2 cups sweet wine (such as Sauterne)
1 teaspoon minced candied ginger

    Scoop the cantaloupe and honeydew melon into balls using a melon baller. Combine the melon balls, wine and ginger in a bowl and toss to coat well. Chill, covered, for 8 to 10 hours. Serve with wooden picks.
    Yield: 6 to 8 servings

Four-Cheese Puffs

1 (1-pound) loaf unsliced white
   bread, crusts trimmed
1/2 cup (1 stick) butter, chopped
1/4 cup shredded mozzarella cheese
1/4 cup shredded sharp Cheddar
   cheese

1/4 cup shredded Swiss cheese
3 ounces cream cheese, softened
1/2 teaspoon dry mustard
1/2 teaspoon salt
1/4 teaspoon cayenne pepper
2 egg whites, stiffly beaten

    Cut the bread into 1-inch cubes; set aside. Mix the butter and cheeses in a saucepan. Cook over medium heat until melted, stirring constantly. Add the mustard, salt and cayenne pepper and mix until blended. Remove from the heat. Fold the egg whites into the cheese mixture. Dip the bread cubes into the cheese mixture using a fondue fork or wooden skewer, coating well on all sides. Place the cubes on a baking sheet. Freeze for 8 to 10 hours. Remove to plastic freezer bags until ready to bake. Place the frozen cubes on a baking sheet. Bake at 400 degrees for 10 to 15 minutes or until golden brown. Serve immediately.
    Yield: 50 puffs

Chinese Sausage Bites

1 pound bulk pork sausage
1 egg, lightly beaten
6 tablespoons bread cubes
3/4 cup bottled chili sauce
6 tablespoons brown sugar

2 tablespoons soy sauce
2 tablespoons vinegar
1/4 teaspoon garlic salt
1/4 cup (1/2 stick) butter

    Crumble the sausage into a large bowl. Add the egg and bread cubes and mix well. Shape into bite-size balls. Brown the meatballs on all sides in a skillet; drain on paper towels. Combine the chili sauce, brown sugar, soy sauce, vinegar, garlic salt and butter in a saucepan. Cook over medium-low heat for 20 minutes, stirring occasionally. Place the meatballs in a serving bowl and pour the hot sauce over the meatballs. Serve immediately with wooden picks.
    Yield: 20 to 25 sausage bites

Cheddar-Stuffed Mushrooms

1 pound whole white mushrooms
6 tablespoons unsalted butter,
   melted
1 onion, finely chopped
1/2 cup chopped fresh parsley

1/2 cup chopped walnuts, toasted
1 cup shredded Cheddar cheese
1/2 cup fresh bread crumbs
1/4 teaspoon salt

Remove the stems from the mushrooms; reserving the stems. Brush the mushroom caps with the melted butter, reserving the butter. Arrange the mushroom caps, stem end up, on a large baking sheet. Finely chop the reserved stems. Sauté the stems and onion in the reserved melted butter in a skillet until softened. Remove from the heat and stir in the parsley, walnuts, Cheddar cheese, bread crumbs and salt. Spoon the mixture into the prepared mushroom caps, mounding slightly. Bake at 350 degrees for 20 minutes. Serve warm.

Yield: 25 servings

Seafood-Stuffed Mushrooms

15 large whole white mushrooms
1 bunch green onions, chopped
   (including tops)
1/2 cup (1 stick) butter
1/2 bag seasoned bread crumbs

1 teaspoon garlic powder
8 ounces cream cheese, softened
1 (6-ounce) can crab meat, drained
1 (4 1/2-ounce) can shrimp, drained
1/2 cup (1 stick) butter, melted

Remove the stems from the mushrooms, reserving the stems. Arrange the mushroom caps, stem end up, in a large greased baking dish. Finely chop the reserved stems. Sauté the stems and green onions in 1/2 cup butter until softened. Pour into a bowl. Add the bread crumbs and garlic powder and mix well. Add the cream cheese and mix well. Stir in the crab meat and shrimp. If the mixture is too thick, add a tablespoon of milk. Spoon the mixture into the mushroom caps, mounding slightly. Bake at 350 degrees for 20 minutes or until golden brown, brushing with 1/2 cup melted butter several times.

Yield: 15 servings

Wild Mushroom Tarts

1 (8-count) package frozen
   tart shells
2 ounces mixed dried or fresh wild
   mushrooms (such as chanterelles,
   morels and porcini)
1 cup hot beef stock
1 onion, chopped
1/4 cup olive oil

1 tablespoon tomato paste
1 cup chopped fresh parsley
2 eggs, beaten
1/2 cup grated Parmesan
   cheese
Salt and pepper to taste
Fresh parsley for garnish
Paprika for garnish

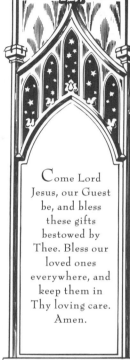

Bake the tart shells in the metal containers in the oven according to the package directions; set aside. If the mushrooms are dried, soak them in the hot beef stock to soften. Remove the mushrooms from the stock, reserving the stock. Cut the mushrooms into strips; set aside. If the mushrooms are fresh, cut into strips and set aside.

Sauté the onion in the olive oil in a large skillet until softened. Add the tomato paste and cook until the paste begins to brown slightly. Add the prepared mushrooms, beef stock and parsley and cook on low for a few minutes or until the mixture thickens. Remove from the heat and let cool until the mixture is lukewarm. Add the eggs, Parmesan cheese, salt and pepper and mix well.

Spoon the mixture into the prepared tart shells. Place the shells in a baking dish. Bake in a water bath at 350 degrees for 1 hour or until set. Remove from the metal cups before serving. Garnish with chopped fresh parsley and paprika.

Note: For a source for dried mushrooms: Delftree Farm, 1-800-243-3742.

Yield: 8 servings

Come Lord Jesus, our Guest be, and bless these gifts bestowed by Thee. Bless our loved ones everywhere, and keep them in Thy loving care. Amen.

Crispy Cheese Straws

2 cups shredded Cheddar cheese
1 cup (2 sticks) margarine, softened
2 cups flour

1/4 teaspoon cayenne pepper
2 cups crisp rice cereal

Combine the Cheddar cheese and margarine in a large bowl and mix well. Add the flour and cayenne pepper and mix until well combined. Stir in the cereal. Spoon into a cookie press and press into straws onto a baking sheet. Bake at 350 degrees for 10 to 12 minutes. Let cool before serving or storing in an airtight container. You may also shape the dough into 1 1/2-inch balls, place on a baking sheet and flatten slightly with a fork to bake.

Yield: 2 dozen

Ice Box Cheese Wafers

2 cups shredded sharp Cheddar
   cheese
1/2 cup (1 stick) butter, softened
1/2 teaspoon salt

1/4 teaspoon cayenne pepper
1 1/2 cups flour
Pecan halves (optional)

Cream the Cheddar cheese, butter, salt and cayenne pepper in a large mixing bowl. Add the flour and mix well. Shape into a log. Wrap in waxed paper and chill until ready to bake. You may also freeze and thaw before baking if desired. Slice thinly, top with a pecan half if desired, and place on an ungreased baking sheet. Bake at 325 degrees for 12 to 15 minutes. Let cool before serving.

Yield: 2 dozen

Vegetable Squares

1 (8-count) can crescent rolls
16 ounces light cream cheese
1/2 cup light sour cream
3/4 cup light mayonnaise
1 envelope ranch salad dressing mix

3/4 cup chopped cauliflower florets
3/4 cup chopped broccoli florets
3/4 cup chopped green onions
3/4 cup chopped tomatoes, drained
3/4 cup shredded Cheddar cheese

Unroll the crescent roll dough onto a 10×15-inch baking pan; press to seal the perforations. Bake at 375 degrees for 8 minutes; let cool. Combine the cream cheese, sour cream, mayonnaise and dressing mix in a bowl and mix until blended. Spread over the cooled crust. Combine the vegetables and Cheddar cheese in a bowl and toss to mix. Sprinkle over the prepared crust. Chill until ready to serve.
Yield: 25 servings

Cajun Snacks

2 2/3 cups each rice, wheat, corn
    and Crispix cereal
2 cups bite-size pretzels
1 1/2 cups French-fried onion rings
1 cup bite-size cheese crackers
1 cup mixed nuts
1/2 cup plus 3 tablespoons
    (1 1/3 sticks) butter, melted
2 tablespoons Worcestershire sauce

1 to 2 teaspoons lemon juice
2 tablespoons parsley flakes
10 drops Tabasco sauce
1 to 2 teaspoons cayenne pepper
1 1/2 teaspoons celery salt
1 1/2 teaspoons garlic powder
1 1/2 teaspoons chili powder
1/2 teaspoon onion powder

Combine the cereal, pretzels, onion rings, cheese crackers and nuts in a large sealable plastic bag. Mix the butter, Worcestershire sauce, lemon juice, parsley flakes, Tabasco sauce and spices in a bowl. Pour the butter mixture into the bag, secure the top and shake gently until the dry ingredients are coated. Pour into a large roasting pan. Bake at 325 degrees for 25 minutes, stirring every 10 minutes. Let cool on paper towels. Store in an airtight container.
Yield: 12 to 14 servings

Artichoke and Jack Dip with Pita Chips

Dip
1/3 cup mayonnaise
8 ounces cream cheese, softened
1/4 teaspoon garlic salt
4 to 5 drops Tabasco sauce
1 1/2 cups shredded Monterey Jack
   cheese
1 (14-ounce) can artichoke hearts,
   drained, chopped
1/2 medium tomato, chopped,
   drained
2 tablespoons chopped green onions
1/2 cup shredded Monterey Jack
   cheese

Pita Chips
1/2 cup (1 stick) butter, melted
1 tablespoon taco seasoning mix
3 (6-inch) pita bread rounds

For the dip, beat the mayonnaise, cream cheese, garlic salt and Tabasco sauce in a mixing bowl for 1 to 2 minutes or until smooth. Stir in 1 1/2 cups Monterey Jack cheese and the artichoke hearts. Spread the mixture in a 9-inch pie plate. Sprinkle with the tomato, green onions and 1/2 cup Monterey Jack cheese. Bake at 375 degrees for 12 to 15 minutes or until bubbly. Serve with the pita chips.

For the pita chips, combine the melted butter and seasoning mix in a small bowl and mix well. Cut each pita round into 6 wedges. Separate each wedge in half to make 36 wedges. Brush both sides with the butter mixture and place on a baking sheet; do not overlap. Bake at 375 degrees for 8 minutes. Turn each wedge over and bake for 2 to 5 minutes longer or until golden brown and crisp.

Yield: 18 servings

Carolina Caviar

1 (15-ounce) can hominy, drained
2 (15-ounce) cans black-eyed
   peas, drained
2 tomatoes, chopped
1 onion, chopped
1 bell pepper, chopped

1 jalapeño chile,
   chopped
2 garlic cloves, minced
1 (8-ounce) bottle
   Italian salad dressing

Combine the hominy, peas, tomatoes, onion, bell pepper, jalapeño and garlic in a serving bowl and mix well. Pour the dressing over the vegetables and toss to coat well. Chill, covered, for 8 to 10 hours. Serve with tortilla chips or crackers.
Yield: 15 servings

Caviar Pie

8 ounces cream cheese, softened
1/2 carton sour cream
3 tablespoons mayonnaise
Grated onion to taste
Tabasco sauce to taste

2 (2-ounce) jars caviar
   (1 red and
   1 black if desired)
Grated hard-cooked egg
   to taste

Beat the cream cheese, sour cream, mayonnaise, onion and Tabasco sauce in a bowl until well blended. Spread in a lightly greased pie plate. Chill, covered, for 8 to 10 hours. Invert onto a serving plate. Place a foil collar around the spread. Top decoratively with the caviar and egg. Remove the foil. Serve with assorted party crackers or toast points.
Yield: 10 to 15 servings

 Richard Pearis, an Englishman and decorated veteran of the French and Indian War, was the first white man to settle in what is now Greenville, SC. With a Cherokee "side wife" and a half-breed son, Pearis was accepted in the Indian world. In 1768, Pearis built a gristmill and a trading post on the falls of the Reedy River. Paris Mountain, a Greenville landmark, was named—albeit with altered spelling— for Pearis.

Hummus

2 cups canned chick-peas
3/4 cup lemon juice
2/3 cup tahini

2 garlic cloves
1 teaspoon salt
Chopped fresh parsley

Combine the chick-peas, lemon juice, tahini, garlic and salt in a food processor or blender container. Process until smooth. Spoon into a serving bowl and top with the parsley. Serve with assorted crackers.

Yield: 15 servings

Layered Taco Dip

1 (16-ounce) can vegetarian
  refried beans
2 cups sour cream
1 envelope taco seasoning mix
2 cups salsa, excess liquid drained

1 to 2 cups shredded Cheddar
  cheese
1 (2-ounce) can sliced black olives,
  drained

Spread the refried beans onto a large serving plate. Combine the sour cream and taco seasoning mix in a small bowl and mix well. Spread over the bean layer. Spread the salsa over the sour cream layer. Sprinkle the Cheddar cheese and olives over the top. Serve with tortilla chips.

Note: The "hint of lime" tortilla chips are especially good. You may use low-fat sour cream and cheese if desired.

Yield: 15 servings

Vidalia Onion Dip

2 cups chopped Vidalia onions
2 cups shredded Swiss cheese
2 cups mayonnaise
Dash of Tabasco sauce

Celery seeds to taste
Dillweed to taste
Paprika to taste

Combine the onions, Swiss cheese, mayonnaise and Tabasco sauce in a bowl and mix well. Pour into a lightly greased baking dish. Sprinkle the celery seeds, dillweed and paprika on top. Bake at 350 degrees for 30 minutes or until bubbly. Serve hot with wheat thins or other assorted crackers.
Yield: 25 servings

Warm Herb Cheese Spread

24 ounces cream cheese, softened
1/4 cup milk
1/4 cup lemon juice
1/2 teaspoon marjoram
1/2 teaspoon basil

1/2 teaspoon oregano
1/2 teaspoon thyme
1/4 teaspoon minced garlic
1 1/2 cups cooked tiny shrimp

Beat the cream cheese in a mixing bowl until smooth and creamy. Beat in the milk and lemon juice, gradually. Add the marjoram, basil, oregano, thyme, garlic and shrimp and stir to mix well. Spoon into a 9-inch quiche or pie plate. Bake, covered, at 350 degrees for 15 to 20 minutes or until bubbly. Serve warm with assorted crackers or fresh vegetables.
Yield: 15 servings

Cream Cheese Ball

16 ounces cream cheese, softened
1 (8-ounce) can crushed pineapple, drained
1 1/4 cups chopped green bell peppers
2 tablespoons finely chopped onion
1 teaspoon seasoned salt
2 cups chopped pecans

Combine the cream cheese, pineapple, bell peppers, onion and seasoned salt in a bowl and mix well. Chill, covered, until firm. Shape into a ball and roll in the pecans to coat well. Serve with assorted crackers. You may also shape into 2 or 3 smaller balls if desired.

Yield: 12 to 15 servings

Smoked Salmon Ball

8 ounces cream cheese, softened
4 ounces smoked salmon, chopped
2 teaspoons fresh lemon juice
1/4 teaspoon freshly ground pepper
1 1/2 tablespoons chopped green onions
1 tablespoon chopped fresh dill

Process the cream cheese in a food processor until creamy. Add the salmon, lemon juice, pepper, green onions and dill and process until the salmon is finely chopped and the mixture is well blended. Shape into a ball. Chill, covered, until firm. Serve with party crackers or bread slices.

Yield: 8 servings

Orange Julius

6 ounces frozen orange juice
    concentrate
1/2 cup milk

1/2 cup water
1/4 cup vanilla ice cream
6 ice cubes

    Combine the orange juice concentrate, milk, water, ice cream and ice cubes in a blender container. Process until smooth. Serve immediately.
    Yield: 2 servings

Eggnog

6 eggs, beaten
2 cups sugar
2 cups milk
4 cups half-and-half

2 tablespoons rum
1 cup bourbon
  (or to taste)
Freshly grated nutmeg

    Beat the eggs and sugar in a mixing bowl until light and lemon-colored. Stir in the milk and pour into a large heavy saucepan. Cook over low heat until 160 degrees on a thermometer, stirring constantly. Remove from the heat and pour through a strainer into a large bowl; let cool. Beat the half-and-half in a small mixing bowl until soft peaks form. Fold into the cooled egg mixture. Stir in the rum and bourbon. Add more milk or half-and-half for desired consistency. Ladle into cups to serve. Sprinkle with freshly grated nutmeg.
    Yield: 18 servings

On a hot Saturday in Anderson, SC, Joe Jackson and his team, the Greenville Spinners, were playing the Anderson Electricians. In the first game, Joe developed blisters on his heels from new shoes, so in the seventh inning of the second game, he removed his shoes to help him run the bases better. After he hit a triple, an Anderson fan yelled out, "You shoeless son-of-a-gun!" Carter "Scoop" Latimer, sports editor of the *Greenville News,* printed the remark the next day, and the name Shoeless Joe Jackson stuck.

Hot Buttered Rum

2 cups (4 sticks) butter, softened
1 (1-pound) package brown sugar
1 (1-pound) package confectioners'
    sugar
2 tablespoons cinnamon
2 teaspoons nutmeg

1 quart natural vanilla
    ice cream, softened
Light rum
Whipped cream
Cinnamon

Combine the butter, brown sugar, confectioners' sugar, 2 tablespoons cinnamon and nutmeg in a large mixing bowl and beat until light and fluffy. Add the ice cream and stir until well blended. Spoon into a 2-quart freezer container; freeze. Keeps well for months in the freezer. To serve, spoon 3 tablespoons of the frozen mixture into a large mug. Add 1 jigger of rum and fill the mug with boiling water. Top with whipped cream and sprinkle with cinnamon. You may also use a cinnamon stick as a stirrer. This is a great holiday treat.

Yield: 20 servings

Irish Cream

1 (14-ounce) can sweetened
    condensed milk
1 cup heavy cream
4 eggs, beaten
1 tablespoon chocolate syrup

1 teaspoon vanilla extract
1 teaspoon instant coffee granules
    dissolved in $1/3$ cup hot water
14 ounces bourbon

Combine the sweetened condensed milk, cream, eggs, chocolate syrup, vanilla, coffee mixture and bourbon in a bowl and mix well. Keep refrigerated and use within 2 days.

Note: To avoid raw eggs that may carry salmonella, use the equivalent amount of pasteurized egg substitute.

Yield: 1 1/2 quarts

Fruit Smoothie

1/2 cup plain or vanilla yogurt
1 tablespoon sugar
1 banana, sliced

Frozen fruit to taste
Milk (optional)

Combine the yogurt, sugar, banana and frozen fruit in a blender container. Process until smooth. Add milk to reach desired consistency.

Note: For the frozen fruit, you may use peaches, strawberries and/or raspberries, or your favorite fruit.

Yield: 2 servings

Hot Mulled Punch

1 (1 1/2-quart) bottle cranberry
  juice
2 (1-quart) bottles apple juice
1/2 cup packed brown sugar

1 1/2 teaspoons whole
  cloves
1/2 teaspoon salt
4 cinnamon sticks

Pour the cranberry juice and apple juice into a 24- to 30-cup percolator or coffeemaker. Combine the brown sugar, cloves, salt and cinnamon sticks in the percolator basket. Perk using the manufacturer's instructions. Serve hot.

Yield: 25 servings

"A county shall be established on the new Ceded Lands by the name of Greeneville," proclaimed the state charter, signed on March 22, 1786. In all probability, Greeneville was named in honor of Revolutionary War general Nathanael Greene.

Brunch & Breads

Breakfast Casserole   26

Egg and Cheese Casserole   26

Fresh Vegetable Frittata   27

Mock Cheese Soufflé   27

Baked Cheese Grits   28

Hash Brown Quiche   28

Crab Quiche   29

McCray Mansion Inn Kiwifruit
   Danish   29

Sour Cream Coffee Cake   30

Butter Pecan Monkey Bread   30

Holiday Morning French Toast   31

Granola   31

Apple Pumpkin Muffins   32

Banana Blueberry Muffins   32

Raspberry Streusel Muffins   33

Hearty Country Muffins   33

Raisin Oat Muffins   34

Tropical Banana Bread   34

Cranberry Bread   35

Orange Date Loaf   35

Dill Bread   36

Irish Soda Bread   36

Popovers   37

Buttermilk Biscuits   37

Cheddar Garlic Biscuits   38

Old-Fashioned Kentucky
   Corn Bread   38

Jalapeño Corn Bread   39

Corn Light Bread   39

Breakfast Casserole

1 1/2 pounds bulk pork sausage
9 eggs, lightly beaten
3 cups milk
1 1/2 teaspoons dry mustard

1 teaspoon salt
3 slices bread, torn into bite-size
   pieces
1 1/2 cups shredded Cheddar cheese

Brown the sausage in a skillet, stirring until crumbly; drain. Combine the eggs, milk, dry mustard and salt in a bowl and mix well with a whisk. Fold in the bread, Cheddar cheese and browned sausage. Pour into a well-greased 9×13-inch baking dish. Chill, covered, for 8 to 10 hours. Bake at 350 degrees for 1 hour. Let stand for 10 to 15 minutes before serving. Serve with fresh fruit and muffins for a delicious, easy breakfast. This is a great Christmas morning dish because you do all the work the night before.

Yield: 12 servings

Egg and Cheese Casserole

1 onion, chopped
2 tablespoons butter
2 tablespoons flour
1 1/4 cups milk
1 cup shredded Cheddar cheese

8 hard-cooked eggs, sliced
8 slices bacon, crisp-cooked,
   crumbled
1 1/2 cups crushed potato chips

Sauté the onion in the butter in a skillet until softened. Add the flour and cook until smooth, stirring constantly. Stir in the milk gradually. Cook until slightly thickened, stirring constantly. Stir in the Cheddar cheese and cook until melted. Remove from the heat. Layer half of the eggs, half of the cheese sauce, half of the bacon and half of the potato chips in a 2-quart baking dish. Repeat the layers. Bake at 350 degrees for 30 minutes. Serve with a green salad and white wine for a nice supper.

Yield: 6 to 8 servings

Fresh Vegetable Frittata

1 large red bell pepper, chopped
1 cup sliced fresh mushrooms
1¹/2 cups shredded Cheddar cheese, divided
1/4 pound cooked asparagus, cut into 1-inch pieces
7 eggs, lightly beaten
1/2 cup mayonnaise
1/2 teaspoon salt
2 tablespoons chopped fresh basil, or 2 teaspoons dried
1 tomato, sliced

Layer the bell pepper, mushrooms and half of the Cheddar cheese in a lightly greased 9-inch deep dish pie plate. Top with the asparagus and remaining cheese. Combine the eggs, mayonnaise, salt and basil in a bowl and mix well with a whisk. Pour evenly over the vegetables and cheese. Top with the tomato slices. Bake at 375 degrees for 35 minutes or until a knife inserted in the center comes out clean. Let stand for 5 minutes before serving. Serve warm.

Yield: 4 to 6 servings

Mock Cheese Soufflé

4 slices white bread, crusts trimmed
Butter
Mustard
2 cups shredded Cheddar cheese
1¹/4 cups milk
2 eggs, beaten
Salt to taste
Paprika to taste

Spread each slice of bread with butter and mustard. Layer the prepared bread slices and Cheddar cheese in a small baking dish. Combine the milk and eggs in a bowl and mix well with a whisk. Pour evenly over the bread and cheese. Let stand for 1 hour or more. Sprinkle with salt and paprika. Bake at 275 degrees for 50 minutes.

Yield: 6 servings

Thank you, Lord, for this food which is set before us. May we use it to nourish our bodies and Thee to our souls. Make us ever more mindful of the needs of others and the needs of our planet. Through Jesus Christ Our Lord.

Baked Cheese Grits

4 cups milk
2 cups water
1 1/2 cups quick-cooking grits
1/2 cup (1 stick) plus
   2 tablespoons butter

1 teaspoon kosher salt
1/2 teaspoon cayenne pepper
1 cup shredded Cheddar cheese
3 eggs, lightly beaten

Combine the milk and water in a large heavy saucepan. Bring to a boil. Add the grits and simmer for 2 to 5 minutes or until thickened, stirring occasionally. Remove from the heat. Stir in the butter, salt, cayenne pepper, Cheddar cheese and eggs until well mixed. Pour into a greased 2-quart baking dish. Bake at 350 degrees for 30 to 40 minutes or until the top is light brown. Serve hot.

Yield: 6 servings

Hash Brown Quiche

3 cups frozen shredded hash brown
   potatoes, thawed
1/3 cup melted butter or margarine
1 cup crumbled crisp-cooked bacon
1 cup shredded Cheddar cheese

1/4 cup chopped green bell pepper
2 eggs
1/2 cup milk
1/2 teaspoon salt
1/4 teaspoon pepper

Press the hash brown potatoes between paper towels to remove the excess moisture. Press over the bottom and up the side of a 9-inch pie plate. Drizzle with the melted butter. Bake at 425 degrees for 25 minutes. Combine the bacon, Cheddar cheese and bell pepper in a bowl. Spoon over the prepared crust. Beat the eggs, milk, salt and pepper in a small mixing bowl until well blended. Pour evenly over the bacon mixture. Bake at 350 degrees for 25 to 30 minutes or until a knife inserted in the center comes out clean. Let stand for 10 minutes before serving.

Yield: 6 servings

Crab Quiche

1 cup mayonnaise
1/4 cup flour
4 eggs, beaten
1 cup milk
6 cups shredded Swiss cheese
2/3 cup sliced green onions

2 cups imitation crab meat,
   or 2 (7-ounce) cans
   flaked crab meat
2 unbaked (9-inch)
   pie shells

Combine the mayonnaise, flour, eggs, milk and Swiss cheese in a bowl and mix well. Fold in the green onions and crab meat. Pour into the pie shells. Bake at 350 degrees for 40 to 45 minutes. Let stand before serving.

Yield: 16 servings

McCray Mansion Inn Kiwifruit Danish

1 (8-count) can crescent rolls
3 ounces cream cheese, softened
1 egg yolk
2 tablespoons sugar

1/2 teaspoon almond extract
2 to 3 kiwifruit, peeled, sliced
1/2 cup apricot jam, warmed

Unroll the crescent rolls and separate into triangles. Beat the cream cheese, egg yolk, sugar and almond extract in a mixing bowl until well blended. Spoon 1 tablespoon of the cream cheese mixture in the center of each triangle and top with a kiwifruit slice. Bring the points of the triangle up to the top and pinch to seal. Place on a baking sheet. Bake at 375 degrees for 12 to 15 minutes. Top with another kiwifruit slice and brush with the warm jam. Serve immediately.

Yield: 8 servings

Located in Greenville is "Broad Margin," one of Frank Lloyd Wright's last designs. Built in 1952 on East Avondale Avenue, it is one of only two Wright-designed houses in South Carolina.

Sour Cream Coffee Cake

1 (2-layer) package yellow or white
   cake mix
3/4 cup vegetable oil
4 eggs

1/2 cup sugar
1 cup sour cream
3 tablespoons brown sugar
1 tablespoon cinnamon

Beat the cake mix, oil, eggs, sugar and sour cream in a large mixing bowl until well blended. Mix the brown sugar and cinnamon in a small bowl. Pour half of the cake batter into a greased and floured bundt pan. Add the brown sugar mixture to the remaining cake batter and mix well; pour into the pan. Bake at 350 degrees for 50 to 60 minutes. Let cool in the pan. Invert onto a plate to serve.

Yield: 16 servings

Butter Pecan Monkey Bread

1/2 cup chopped pecans
24 frozen dinner rolls
1 (6-ounce) package butter pecan
   instant pudding mix

1/2 cup (1 stick) butter, melted
1 cup packed brown sugar
2 tablespoons milk

Sprinkle the pecans over the surface of a buttered bundt pan. Place the frozen rolls in the prepared pan. Sprinkle with the pudding mix. Combine the melted butter, brown sugar and milk and mix well. Pour the mixture over the frozen rolls. Let rise, covered, for 8 to 10 hours. Bake at 350 degrees for 25 minutes. Invert onto a plate to serve.

Yield: 16 servings

Holiday Morning French Toast

1 cup packed brown sugar
1/2 cup (1 stick) butter, melted
3 teaspoons cinnamon
3 tart apples, peeled, cored,
    thinly sliced
1/2 cup dried cranberries

1 loaf French bread,
    cut into 1-inch slices
6 eggs
1 1/2 cups milk
1 tablespoon vanilla extract

Mix the brown sugar, butter and 1 teaspoon of the cinnamon in a bowl. Add the apples and cranberries and toss to coat well. Spread evenly over the bottom of a 9×13-inch baking dish. Arrange the bread slices on top. Beat the eggs, milk, vanilla and remaining 2 teaspoons cinnamon in a mixing bowl until well blended. Pour evenly over the bread. Chill, covered, for 6 to 24 hours. Bake, covered with foil, at 375 degrees for 40 minutes. Uncover and bake for 5 minutes. Let stand for 5 minutes. Serve warm.

Yield: 12 servings

Granola

1 (18-ounce) package rolled oats
2 cups flaked coconut
1 cup chopped walnuts or pecans
1 cup sunflower seed kernels

1 cup sesame seeds
1 1/4 cups honey
1/4 cup extra-light olive oil
1 tablespoon vanilla extract

Combine the oats, coconut, walnuts, sunflower kernels and sesame seeds in a large bowl and mix well. Heat the honey, olive oil and vanilla in a saucepan over medium heat for a few minutes, stirring occasionally. Pour over the oat mixture, tossing to coat well. Spread into a 3-quart baking dish about 1/2 inch thick. Bake at 250 degrees for 45 minutes, stirring every 15 minutes. Increase the heat to 300 degrees and bake until golden brown, stirring occasionally. Let cool. Store in a sealable plastic bags. May freeze if desired.

Yield: 20 servings

Apple Pumpkin Muffins

1 2/3 cups flour
1 cup sugar
1 tablespoon pumpkin pie spice
1 teaspoon baking soda
1/4 teaspoon baking powder

1/4 teaspoon salt
1 cup canned pumpkin
1/2 cup (1 stick) margarine, melted
2 eggs, lightly beaten
1 apple, peeled, finely chopped

Mix the flour, sugar, pumpkin pie spice, baking soda, baking powder and salt in a large bowl. Make a well in the center of the mixture. Beat the pumpkin, melted margarine and eggs in a mixing bowl until well blended. Add to the flour mixture and stir just until moistened. Fold in the apple. Spoon into greased muffin cups, filling 2/3 full. Bake at 350 degrees for 20 minutes. Remove to wire racks to cool.

Yield: 1 dozen

Banana Blueberry Muffins

1 egg
1/2 cup packed brown sugar
4 to 5 ripe bananas, mashed
1/4 cup raisins, soaked in warm
   water, drained
3/4 cup blueberries or nuts
1/3 cup vegetable oil
1 teaspoon vanilla

3/4 cup all-purpose flour
3/4 cup whole wheat flour
1/2 cup oat bran
2 tablespoons baking powder
1/2 teaspoon baking soda
3/4 teaspoon cinnamon
1/4 teaspoon nutmeg
1/4 teaspoon salt

Beat the egg and brown sugar in a bowl with a wooden spoon until light and smooth. Add the bananas, raisins, blueberries, oil and vanilla and beat until well mixed. Combine the all-purpose flour, whole wheat flour, oat bran, baking powder, baking soda, cinnamon, nutmeg and salt in a large bowl. Fold in the banana mixture just until moistened. Spoon into greased muffin cups, filling 2/3 full. Bake at 375 degrees for 20 to 25 minutes. Remove to wire racks to cool.

Yield: 18 muffins

Raspberry Streusel Muffins

1 1/2 cups flour
1/2 cup sugar
2 teaspoons baking powder
1 egg, beaten
1/2 cup milk
1/2 cup (1 stick) butter, melted

1 cup frozen unsweetened
  raspberries
1/4 cup flour
2 tablespoons butter, melted
1/4 cup chopped pecans
1/4 cup packed brown sugar

Mix 1 1/2 cups flour, the sugar and baking powder in a large bowl. Make a well in the center of the mixture. Combine the egg, milk and 1/2 cup melted butter in a bowl and mix well. Add to the flour mixture and stir just until moistened. Fold in the raspberries. Spoon into greased muffin cups, filling 2/3 full. Combine 1/4 cup flour, 2 tablespoons melted butter, the pecans and brown sugar and mix until crumbly. Sprinkle over the batter in each cup. Bake at 375 degrees for 20 to 25 minutes. Remove to wire racks to cool.

Yield: 1 dozen

Hearty Country Muffins

2 1/2 cups flour
1 1/3 cups sugar
1 tablespoon baking powder
2 teaspoons baking soda
2 teaspoons cinnamon
1 teaspoon (or more) freshly grated
  nutmeg

1/2 teaspoon salt
2 eggs, lightly beaten
1/2 cup vegetable oil
2 cups chopped peeled apples
1 cup shredded carrots
1 cup dried cranberries
1 cup chopped pecans

Mix the dry ingredients in a large bowl. Beat the eggs and oil in a mixing bowl until well blended. Mix in the apples, carrots, cranberries and pecans. Add to the flour mixture and stir just until moistened. Let stand for 15 minutes. Spoon into greased muffin cups, filling 3/4 full. Bake at 350 degrees for 20 to 25 minutes. Remove to wire racks to cool. May also bake in mini loaf pans.

Yield: 2 dozen

Raisin Oat Muffins

1 1/2 cups rolled oats
1 1/4 cups flour
3/4 teaspoon cinnamon
1 teaspoon baking powder
3/4 teaspoon baking soda
1 cup unsweetened applesauce

1/2 cup skim milk
1/2 cup packed brown sugar
3 tablespoons vegetable oil
1 egg white, beaten
1/3 to 1/2 cup raisins

Mix the first 5 ingredients in a large bowl. Beat the applesauce, milk, brown sugar, oil and egg white in a mixing bowl until blended. Add to the oat mixture and stir just until moistened. Fold in the raisins. Spoon into greased muffin cups, filling 2/3 full. Bake at 400 degrees for 20 minutes. Cool on wire racks.
 Yield: 1 to 2 dozen

Tropical Banana Bread

1/2 cup golden raisins
1/3 cup rum
1/2 cup (1 stick) unsalted butter, softened
1/2 cup packed brown sugar
1 egg
2 teaspoons vanilla extract
2 cups flour

1 teaspoon baking powder
1/2 teaspoon each baking soda and salt
1 teaspoon freshly grated nutmeg
1 teaspoon ground ginger
3 very ripe bananas, mashed
2/3 cup chopped toasted macadamia nuts
1/2 cup flaked coconut

Simmer the raisins and rum in a small saucepan for 10 minutes. Let cool. Beat the butter and brown sugar in a mixing bowl until light and fluffy. Beat in the egg and vanilla. Sift the dry ingredients together. Add to the butter mixture alternately with the mashed bananas, beating well after each addition. Fold in the macadamia nuts, coconut and raisin-rum mixture. Pour into a greased and floured 5×9-inch loaf pan. Bake at 350 degrees for 1 hour or until tests done; do not overbake. Let cool in the pan for 30 minutes. Remove to a wire rack.
 Yield: 12 servings

Cranberry Bread

2 cups flour
1 cup sugar
1 1/2 teaspoons baking powder
1/2 teaspoon baking soda
1/2 teaspoon salt
1 egg, beaten

Grated zest of 1 orange
2 tablespoons hot water
2 tablespoons shortening
1/2 cup orange juice
1 cup fresh cranberries, sliced
1/2 cup (or more) chopped pecans

Combine the flour, sugar, baking powder, baking soda and salt in a large bowl. Add the egg, orange zest, hot water, shortening and orange juice and beat well. Fold in the cranberries and pecans. Spoon into a greased and floured loaf pan. Bake at 325 degrees for 1 hour or until a wooden pick inserted in the center comes out clean. This makes a nice gift to give around the holidays.

Yield: 12 servings

Orange Date Loaf

2 cups flour
1 1/2 teaspoons baking powder
1/2 teaspoon baking soda
1/2 cup hot water
2/3 cup chopped dates
1 orange, cut into 8 segments

1 egg
2 tablespoons butter, softened
1/2 teaspoon salt
3/4 cup sugar
1/2 to 3/4 cup chopped nuts

Sift the flour, baking powder and baking soda into a large mixing bowl. Combine the hot water and dates in a food processor container. Process until well blended. Add the orange and process. Add the egg, butter, salt and sugar and process until well blended. Add the nuts and process, but do not grind the nuts very fine. Fold into the flour mixture and stir until well mixed. Spoon into a greased loaf pan. Bake at 350 degrees for 1 hour or until a wooden pick inserted in the center comes out clean.

Yield: 12 servings

Dill Bread

1 envelope dry yeast
1/4 cup warm water
1 cup cottage cheese
2 tablespoons sugar
1 tablespoon minced onion
1 tablespoon butter

1 teaspoon dillseed
1/4 teaspoon baking soda
1 teaspoon salt
1 egg, beaten
2 1/4 cups flour
Butter

Dissolve the yeast in the warm water in a large bowl. Add the cottage cheese, sugar, onion, 1 tablespoon butter, dillseed, baking soda, salt, egg and flour and mix well. Let rise, covered, for 1 hour or until doubled in bulk. Punch down and stir. Place in a round baking dish. Bake at 350 degrees for 40 to 45 minutes or until light brown. Brush the top of the bread with butter while hot.

Yield: 12 servings

Irish Soda Bread

3 cups flour
1/2 cup sugar
1 tablespoon baking powder
1 teaspoon salt
1/2 teaspoon baking soda

1 cup raisins
1 tablespoon caraway seeds
1 1/2 cups buttermilk
1/4 cup (1/2 stick) butter or
    margarine, melted

Combine the flour, sugar, baking powder, salt and baking soda in a bowl. Stir in the raisins and caraway seeds. Mix in the buttermilk and melted butter with a fork until moistened. Place in a greased round baking dish and cut an "X" in the top of the dough with a knife. Bake at 350 degrees for 1 hour and 10 minutes or until a wooden pick inserted near the center comes out clean.

Yield: 16 to 18 servings

Popovers

3 eggs
1 cup milk
1 cup flour

1/2 teaspoon salt
1 tablespoon butter or
    margarine, melted

   Beat the eggs, milk, flour, salt and melted butter in a mixing bowl until smooth. Pour the batter into greased muffin cups or ovenproof custard cups, filling 1/3 full. Bake at 400 degrees for 35 minutes or until crisp and golden brown.
   Yield: 10 servings

Buttermilk Biscuits

2 cups flour
1/2 teaspoon baking soda
1/2 teaspoon salt

3 tablespoons shortening
3/4 cup buttermilk
Melted butter (optional)

   Combine the flour, baking soda and salt in a bowl. Cut in the shortening until crumbly. Add the buttermilk and stir until moistened. Turn onto a floured surface and knead 3 or 4 times. Shape the dough into small balls and place on a baking sheet. You may also roll the dough on a floured surface to a 1/2-inch thickness and cut with a 2-inch biscuit cutter. Bake at 450 degrees for 12 to 15 minutes. Brush with melted butter if desired.
   Yield: 1 dozen

 In 1797, land baron Lemuel J. Alston founded Greeneville County's first village. He called it Pleasantburg, but the name never caught on. In 1831, the village was officially incorporated by the General Assembly as Greenville.

Cheddar Garlic Biscuits

2 cups baking mix
2/3 cup milk
1/2 cup shredded Cheddar cheese

2 tablespoons melted butter
1/4 teaspoon garlic powder

Combine the baking mix, milk and Cheddar cheese in a bowl and stir to form a soft dough. Drop by spoonfuls onto a baking sheet. Bake at 450 degrees for 8 to 10 minutes. Mix the melted butter and garlic powder in a small bowl. Brush over the warm biscuits.

Yield: 10 servings

Old-Fashioned Kentucky Corn Bread

1 1/2 cups white cornmeal
1 1/2 teaspoons salt
1 teaspoon baking powder
2 eggs, lightly beaten

1 1/4 cups buttermilk
2 tablespoons melted shortening
Shortening

Combine the cornmeal, salt and baking powder in a mixing bowl. Add the eggs, buttermilk and 2 tablespoons melted shortening and beat well. Place a small amount of shortening in each section of a cast-iron corn bread mold. Heat the mold in a 450-degree oven. Pour the batter into each section of the hot mold. Bake at 450 degrees for 20 minutes.

Yield: 8 servings

Jalapeño Corn Bread

3 eggs, beaten
2 1/4 cups milk
1/2 cup vegetable oil
3 cups corn bread mix
3 teaspoons sugar
1 large onion, grated

1 teaspoon baking powder
1 (20-ounce) can cream-style corn
3 jalapeño chiles, finely chopped
2 cups shredded sharp Cheddar
   cheese

Beat the eggs, milk and oil in a mixing bowl. Add the corn bread mix, sugar, onion, baking powder, corn, chiles and Cheddar cheese and mix well. Pour into a large baking dish or 2 smaller dishes. Bake at 375 degrees for 40 to 45 minutes. This is delicious served with soup.

Yield: 12 to 16 servings

Corn Light Bread

2 cups cornmeal
1 cup flour
1 teaspoon salt
1/4 cup sugar
1 teaspoon baking soda

1 teaspoon baking powder
2 cups buttermilk
1 egg, beaten
1/2 cup vegetable oil

Combine the cornmeal, flour, salt, sugar, baking soda and baking powder in a large bowl. Make a well in the center of the mixture. Beat the buttermilk, egg and oil in a mixing bowl until well blended. Add to the cornmeal mixture and mix quickly just until moistened. Pour into a greased loaf pan. Bake at 350 degrees for 1 hour.

Yield: 12 servings

Soups & Salads

Chilled Peach Soup

2 cups sliced peaches
1 cup white wine
1 cup vanilla yogurt
1/2 cup sugar

1/2 cup sour cream
1 teaspoon lemon juice
Peach slices for garnish
Lemon thyme for garnish

Combine the peaches, wine, yogurt, sugar, sour cream and lemon juice in a blender container. Process until smooth. Refrigerate, covered, until chilled. Ladle into bowls to serve. Garnish with sliced peaches and chopped fresh lemon thyme.

Yield: 4 servings

Barbara Bush's Chilled Zucchini Soup

1 pound zucchini
2 tablespoons chopped shallots
   (may also use onion or leeks)
1 garlic clove, minced
1 3/4 cups chicken broth

1 teaspoon curry powder
1/2 teaspoon salt
1/2 cup cream
Chopped chives for garnish

Chop the zucchini; do not peel. Combine the zucchini, shallots, garlic and chicken broth in a large heavy skillet. Bring to a boil, reduce the heat and simmer for 10 to 20 minutes, stirring frequently. Pour the zucchini mixture into a blender container. Add the curry powder and salt. Process until the mixture is puréed. Add the cream and process until well blended. Pour into a bowl. Chill, covered, until serving time. Ladle into bowls. Serve cold garnished with chopped chives.

Yield: 6 servings

Borscht

1 (15-ounce) can julienned beets
1/2 teaspoon MSG
1/2 teaspoon salt
Dash of pepper

1 tablespoon grated onion
Grated zest and juice of 1 lemon
1 (14 1/2-ounce) can beef broth
Sour cream

Combine the beets, MSG, salt, pepper, onion, lemon zest and juice in a blender container. Process until smooth. Add the beef broth and process until well blended. Chill, covered, for 8 to 10 hours. Stir well before serving. Ladle into bowls to serve. Top with a dollop of sour cream.

Yield: 4 servings

Arizona Mountain Soup

1 1/2 cups dried pinto beans
3 cups water
3 slices bacon, chopped
2 medium onions, finely chopped
2 garlic cloves, minced
1 (16-ounce) can chopped tomatoes

1 1/2 cups cooked brown rice
2 teaspoons salt
1/4 teaspoon paprika
1/4 teaspoon pepper
2 cups water

Sort and rinse the beans. Soak the beans in 3 cups water in a large saucepan, covered, for 8 to 10 hours. Do not drain. Bring to a boil, reduce the heat and simmer, covered, for 2 hours or until the beans are tender. Drain, reserving the liquid. Cook the bacon in a Dutch oven over medium heat until almost crisp. Add the onions and garlic and cook until tender, stirring frequently. Add the prepared beans, tomatoes, rice, salt, paprika and pepper. Stir in the reserved bean liquid and 2 cups water. Bring to a boil, reduce the heat and simmer, covered, for 1 hour, stirring occasionally.

Yield: 6 servings

Bourbon Onion Soup Flambé

4 cups thinly sliced onions
2 garlic cloves, minced
4 tablespoons butter
6 cups chicken broth
Salt to taste
Pepper to taste

12 thin slices French bread, toasted
4 slices Swiss cheese
Freshly grated Parmesan cheese
Paprika to taste
4 ounces (about) bourbon

Sauté the onions and garlic in the butter in a large stockpot until softened. Add the chicken broth and simmer for 20 minutes. Season with salt and pepper. Ladle the soup into 4 ovenproof bowls. Place 3 slices of bread in each bowl. Place the Swiss cheese slices on top of the bread in each bowl. Sprinkle generously with the Parmesan cheese and sprinkle the top lightly with the paprika. Spray the top with olive oil cooking spray. Place the bowls in a baking dish filled with 1/2 inch of water. Bake at 425 degrees for 20 minutes or until the cheese is brown and bubbly. Immediately before serving, spoon about 1 ounce of bourbon on top of each bowl and ignite with a kitchen lighter.

Yield: 4 servings

Potato Cream Cheese Soup

3 1/3 pounds potatoes
1 large onion
Chicken broth
2 tablespoons salt
Pepper to taste

1/4 cup (1/2 stick) butter
8 ounces cream cheese
Milk
Chopped chives

Chop the potatoes and onion and cook in a mixture of water and chicken broth to cover in a stockpot until the potatoes are tender. Stir in the salt and pepper. Cut the butter and cream cheese into pieces. Add to the pot and cook until melted. Add milk to reach the desired consistency. Cook until heated through. Ladle into bowls to serve. Top with chopped chives.

Yield: 4 to 6 servings

Black Bean Soup

1 pound dried black beans
2 tablespoons olive oil
1/2 cup salt pork, cut into strips
2 smoked ham hocks
2 cups chopped onions
3 garlic cloves, minced
7 cups chicken broth

Salt to taste
Black pepper to taste
1/4 teaspoon cayenne pepper
1 tablespoon red wine vinegar
1/4 cup dry sherry
Hot cooked rice
Chopped onion (optional)

Rinse and sort the beans. Soak in cold water to cover in a bowl for 8 to 10 hours. Heat the olive oil in a 6-quart stockpot. Sauté the salt pork, ham hocks, onions and garlic until the onions and garlic are softened.

Rinse and drain the beans. Add the beans and chicken broth to the pot; bring to a boil. Stir in the salt, black pepper and cayenne pepper. Reduce the heat and simmer, partially covered, for 2 to 4 hours or until the beans are tender, stirring occasionally.

Remove the salt pork and ham hocks, leaving the small pieces of ham and pork. Strain to remove about 1/3 of the beans. Purée in a food processor or blender and return to the soup mixture. Stir in the red wine vinegar and sherry. Cook until heated through. Ladle into bowls over the rice. Top with chopped onion if desired. This soup is easy to double and fun to serve to a crowd.

Yield: 6 servings

Our Dear Heavenly Father, we thank Thee for this food. Feed our souls on the bread of life and help us to do our part in kind words and loving deeds. We ask in Jesus' name. Amen.

Venison and Black Bean Chili

2 tablespoons olive oil
2 pounds venison stew meat,
   cut into 1-inch cubes
1 tablespoon olive oil
2 large onions, chopped
4 slices bacon, cut into
   1/4-inch pieces
8 garlic cloves, minced
2 large red bell peppers, chopped
2 jalapeño chiles, seeded, chopped
1/4 cup chili powder
2 tablespoons cumin
1/4 teaspoon cayenne pepper

Salt to taste
Black pepper to taste
1 (15-ounce) can diced tomatoes
1 (6-ounce) can tomato paste
1 (14-ounce) can chicken broth
1 1/2 cups dry red wine
1 cup water
2 (15-ounce) cans black beans,
   rinsed, drained
Sour cream
Shredded Cheddar cheese
Scallions
Lime wedges

Heat 2 tablespoons olive oil in a large Dutch oven until very hot but not smoking. Brown the venison in the oil in batches, adding additional oil if necessary; drain, reserving the drippings. Remove the venison to a bowl. Add 1 tablespoon olive oil to the Dutch oven and sauté the onions, bacon and garlic over medium heat for 6 to 8 minutes or until the onions are tender.

Add the bell peppers and jalapeños to the Dutch oven and cook an additional 4 to 5 minutes, stirring frequently. Stir in the chili powder, cumin, cayenne pepper, salt and black pepper and cook 1 minute or until the spices are fragrant. Add the undrained tomatoes, tomato paste, chicken broth, wine, water, venison and reserved drippings. Bring to a boil, stirring frequently.

Reduce the heat and simmer, covered, for 1 1/2 hours, stirring occasionally. Add the black beans and simmer for 10 minutes. Serve with sour cream, shredded Cheddar cheese, scallions and lime wedges. This is great for Super Bowl parties.

Yield: 8 to 10 servings

Cincinnati Chili

2 tablespoons butter
2 pounds ground beef
6 bay leaves
1 large onion, finely chopped
6 garlic cloves, minced
4 teaspoons vinegar
2 teaspoons allspice
2 teaspoons cayenne pepper
1 1/2 teaspoons salt
1 teaspoon cumin
1 teaspoon cinnamon
1 teaspoon dried whole red pepper,
   crushed
1/2 teaspoon oregano
   (preferably Mexican)

1 (6-ounce) can tomato
   paste
6 cups water
1 (16-ounce) can kidney
   beans, drained
   (for 5-Way Chili)
8 ounces vermicelli,
   cooked, drained
8 ounces shredded
   Cheddar cheese
1 small onion, finely
   chopped (for 4-Way
   and 5-Way Chili)

Heat the butter in a large heavy skillet over medium-high heat. Add the ground beef. Brown the ground beef, stirring until crumbly. Stir in the bay leaves, onion, garlic, vinegar, allspice, cayenne pepper, salt, cumin, cinnamon, red pepper, oregano, tomato paste and water. You may adjust the seasonings to taste. Bring to a boil, reduce the heat and simmer for 2 to 4 hours.

For 5-Way Chili, add the kidney beans 30 minutes before serving. Remove the bay leaves. To serve, spoon a small amount of the cooked vermicelli into each bowl. Ladle a generous amount of chili on top. Top with the shredded Cheddar cheese. For 4-Way or 5-Way Chili, top with the finely chopped onion.

Yield: 10 servings

Mexican Chicken Soup

1 (3- to 3 1/2-pound) chicken
6 cups water
3 ribs celery
1 onion, chopped
Salt and pepper to taste
3 carrots, thinly sliced

1 tablespoon plus 4 teaspoons
  chicken bouillon granules
1 onion, chopped
1 (16-ounce) can chopped tomatoes
1 zucchini, thinly sliced
1 cup frozen English peas

Combine the chicken, water, celery, 1 onion, salt and pepper in a Dutch oven. Bring to a boil. Reduce the heat and simmer, covered, for 1 hour. Remove the chicken and let cool. Cut the chicken into bite-size pieces, discarding the skin and bones. Strain the cooking liquid, discarding the vegetables. Return the broth to the Dutch oven. Add the carrots, bouillon, 1 onion and tomatoes. Simmer, covered, for 35 to 45 minutes. Add the chicken, zucchini and peas. Simmer, covered, for 25 minutes. You may also add frozen mixed vegetables, rice or spaghetti. It is easy to double and also freezes well.
Yield: 10 servings

West African Chicken Peanut Stew

1 quart chicken broth, heated,
  halved
3/4 cup creamy peanut butter
2 tablespoons butter or margarine

6 tablespoons flour
2 1/2 cups chopped cooked chicken
Salt and pepper to taste
3 tablespoons vermouth

Combine half of the chicken broth and the peanut butter in a bowl and mix until smooth. Melt the butter in a saucepan. Add the flour and remaining chicken broth and whisk until smooth. Simmer for 5 minutes. Add the peanut butter mixture and chicken. Cook until heated through, stirring occasionally. Season with salt and pepper. Stir in the vermouth immediately before serving. Ladle into bowls and garnish with cooked rice, sliced banana, chopped peanuts, hard-cooked egg, raisins, chutney, grapefruit or orange sections.
Yield: 4 to 6 servings

Wild Rice and Mushroom Turkey Soup

1 turkey carcass
2 ribs celery, with leaves
2 carrots, halved
1 onion, quartered
1 bay leaf
1 tablespoon thyme
2 teaspoons sage
1 bunch fresh parsley
1/2 ounce dried wild mushrooms
    (such as porcini or shiitake)
8 cups water
3 tablespoons unsalted butter
2 leeks, white and light green
    parts, halved lengthwise,
    thinly sliced, rinsed

2 ribs celery, thinly sliced
2 carrots, thinly sliced
1 1/2 cups sliced mixed mushrooms
    (such as button, shiitake or
    cremini)
Kosher salt to taste
Freshly ground pepper to taste
2 cups chopped cooked turkey
1 cup cooked wild rice
1/4 cup crème fraîche or sour cream
2 tablespoons chopped fresh chives
    or thinly sliced scallions

Combine the turkey carcass, 2 ribs celery, 2 halved carrots, onion, bay leaf, thyme, sage, parsley, wild mushrooms and water in a large stockpot. Simmer for 2 to 3 hours. Strain, reserving the broth. Add the butter to the stockpot and melt over medium heat. Add the leeks, sliced celery and sliced carrots and cook for 10 minutes or until tender, stirring occasionally. Stir in the 1 1/2 cups mushrooms and cook until tender. Season with the salt and pepper. Add the reserved broth and turkey and mix well.

Simmer for 15 minutes, stirring occasionally. Add the wild rice and cook an additional 5 minutes. You may adjust the seasonings to taste. Ladle into warm bowls and serve with a dollop of crème fraîche. Sprinkle with the chives.

Yield: 6 servings

Corn and Crab Soup

3 to 4 small red potatoes
2 cups chicken broth
1 1/2 cups corn kernels
1 bay leaf
3 tablespoons butter

3 tablespoons flour
2 cups (or more) milk
6 ounces imitation crab meat, flaked
1/8 teaspoon cayenne pepper
2 to 3 drops hot pepper sauce

Peel and chop the potatoes. Cook the potatoes, broth, corn and bay leaf in a medium saucepan over medium heat for 10 minutes or until the potatoes are tender. Melt the butter in a saucepan. Stir in the flour and milk. Cook until thickened and bubbly, stirring frequently. Add the potato mixture. Stir in the crab meat, cayenne and hot pepper sauce and cook until heated through. May add more milk and adjust the seasonings. Remove the bay leaf.

Yield: 4 to 6 servings

Fish Chowder

6 slices bacon
1 large onion, chopped
3 ribs celery, chopped
4 potatoes, chopped
3 cups water
2 cups fish broth or bouillon

1 pound firm white fish, cut into
    bite-size pieces
1 cup nonfat dry milk powder
3 tablespoons flour
1 cup cold water
Salt and pepper to taste

Cook the bacon in a large heavy skillet until crisp. Crumble the bacon into a bowl; set aside. Sauté the onion and celery in the bacon drippings until softened. Add the potatoes and water. Bring to a boil and cook until the potatoes are tender. Bring the fish broth to a boil in a saucepan. Add the fish and cook until the fish flakes easily. Add to the potato mixture and simmer for 20 minutes. Combine the dry milk powder, flour and water in a bowl and mix until well blended. Add to the soup and simmer until thickened. Add the salt and pepper and mix well. Ladle into bowls to serve. Top with the crumbled bacon.

Yield: 4 to 6 servings

Seafood Gumbo

2 1/2 cups flour
1 tablespoon olive oil
2 cups chopped celery
1 cup chopped green bell pepper
1 cup chopped onion
1 cup chopped green onions
5 garlic cloves, minced
1 tablespoon filé powder
7 (14 1/2-ounce) cans no-salt-added fat-free chicken broth
1 tablespoon salt
1/2 teaspoon pepper
1/2 teaspoon cayenne pepper
1 tablespoon hot pepper sauce
1 (10-ounce) package frozen chopped okra
3 pounds shrimp, peeled, deveined
2 pounds crab meat, drained, picked over
2 (12-ounce) containers oysters (do not drain the liquor)
Hot cooked rice

Sprinkle the flour evenly into a 10×15-inch baking pan. Bake at 400 degrees for 20 minutes, stirring frequently; do not burn. Let cool. Heat the olive oil in a large stockpot over medium heat. Add the celery, bell pepper, onion, green onions, garlic and filé powder. Sauté for 5 to 7 minutes or until tender. Mix in the toasted flour, chicken broth, salt, pepper, cayenne and hot pepper sauce.

Bring to a boil, reduce the heat and simmer for 30 minutes. Add the okra and simmer for 30 minutes. Add the shrimp, crab meat and oysters. Cook for 5 minutes. Serve over hot cooked rice.

Yield: 24 servings

Frank Selvy scored 100 points in a basketball game between Furman University and Newberry College during the 1953–54 season. The game was played in the old Textile Hall building on Greenville's West Washington Street. Selvy holds the Southern Conference season scoring record for 41.7 points per game during the 1953–54 season. He also holds the conference career scoring record with an average of 32.5 per game 1950–1954.

Chart House Bleu Cheese Dressing

3/4 cup sour cream
1 teaspoon Worcestershire sauce
1/2 teaspoon each dry mustard,
    pepper, salt and garlic powder

1 1/2 cups mayonnaise
4 ounces imported Danish bleu
    cheese, crumbled

    Process the sour cream, Worcestershire sauce and spices in a blender on low for 2 minutes. Add the mayonnaise and process on low for 30 seconds. Increase the speed to medium and process for 2 minutes. Add the bleu cheese and process on low for 4 minutes. Chill, covered, for 24 hours before serving.
    Yield: 2 1/2 cups

Caesar Salad

Caesar Dressing
3/4 cup olive oil
1/2 garlic clove, crushed
1 1/2 teaspoons salt
1/2 teaspoon dry mustard
Freshly ground pepper to taste
1 coddled egg
3 tablespoons wine vinegar

Salad
1 loaf Italian bread, cubed
2 heads romaine
Freshly grated Parmesan cheese

    For the dressing, combine the olive oil and garlic in a bowl and let stand for 30 minutes. Reserve 1/4 cup of the oil mixture for the croutons. Combine the remaining oil mixture, salt, dry mustard, pepper and egg in a blender. Process until well blended. Add the vinegar and process for a few seconds. Chill.
    For the salad, toss the reserved 1/4 cup oil mixture with the bread cubes in a bowl. Spread the bread cubes on a baking sheet. Bake at 200 degrees for 1 hour, stirring after 30 minutes. Tear the romaine into bite-size pieces into a large salad bowl. Add the prepared croutons and Parmesan cheese to the salad bowl. Pour the dressing over the top and toss to mix well. Serve immediately.
    Yield: 8 servings

Korean Salad

Korean Dressing
1/2 cup salad oil
1/4 cup sugar
1 small onion, chopped
1 tablespoon Worcestershire sauce

Salad
1 bunch spinach, torn
1 (16-ounce) can bean sprouts,
    drained
1 (8-ounce) can water chestnuts,
    drained, sliced
5 slices bacon, crisp-cooked, crumbled
2 hard-cooked eggs, sliced

For the dressing, combine the salad oil, sugar, onion and Worcestershire sauce in a blender and process until blended. Chill until serving time.

For the salad, combine the spinach, bean sprouts, water chestnuts, bacon and eggs in a large salad bowl. Pour the dressing over the top and toss to mix well.

Yield: 4 servings

Baby Greens with Macadamia Nuts

2 (31/2-ounce) logs soft goat cheese
1/2 cup finely chopped macadamia
    nuts
8 cups mixed baby greens

1 avocado, cut into thin wedges
8 tablespoons olive oil
3 tablespoons balsamic vinegar
Salt and pepper to taste

Slice each goat cheese log into 6 rounds. Press the cheese rounds into the nuts, turning to coat both sides; chill, covered. Reserve the remaining nuts. Place the cheese rounds on a plate. Mound the greens in a large salad bowl. Arrange the avocado slices on top of the greens. Whisk 6 tablespoons olive oil and vinegar in a small bowl. Season with the salt and pepper. Chill until serving time. Heat 2 tablespoons olive oil in a large non-stick skillet over medium heat. Add the cheese rounds and sauté for 1 minute or until warmed through, but not melted. Arrange the cheese rounds on top of the salad. Drizzle with the prepared dressing. Sprinkle with the remaining nuts. Toss and serve immediately.

Yield: 4 servings

Warm Walnut Salad with Orange Raspberry Dressing

Orange Raspberry Dressing
2 teaspoons butter
1 leek, sliced into 1/4-inch pieces
1/2 cup walnuts, coarsely chopped
3 tablespoons walnut oil
2 tablespoons raspberry vinegar
Grated zest of 1 orange

Salad
1 head butter lettuce
1 head radicchio
2 ounces goat cheese, crumbled
Salt to taste
Pepper to taste

For the dressing, heat the butter in a skillet over medium-high heat. Add the leek and sauté for 3 minutes or until softened. Add the walnuts and sauté for 2 minutes. Remove from the heat. Immediately stir in the walnut oil, vinegar and orange zest. Let stand for 20 seconds or until heated through.

For the salad, combine the greens in a salad bowl. Top with the goat cheese. Pour the warm dressing over the salad. Season with salt and pepper; toss.

Yield: 4 servings

Spinach Salad

Sweet and Sour Dressing
1 cup salad oil
1/2 cup vinegar
1/2 cup sugar
1/2 cup ketchup
1 teaspoon salt
1/2 teaspoon Worcestershire sauce

Salad
1 pound spinach, torn
1/2 pound bacon, crisp-cooked
1 small onion, chopped
1 (16-ounce) can bean sprouts
1/2 cup shredded Swiss cheese
4 hard-cooked eggs, sliced

For the dressing, process all the ingredients in a blender until well blended. You may also mix well with a whisk in a bowl. Chill until serving time.

For the salad, combine the spinach, bacon, onion, drained sprouts, cheese and eggs in a large salad bowl and toss to mix well. Add the dressing; toss to coat.

Yield: 4 to 6 servings

Seven-Layer Salad

Leaf lettuce, torn into bite-size
  pieces
1 pound bacon, crisp-cooked,
  crumbled
6 hard-cooked eggs, sliced
Spinach, torn into bite-size pieces
2 to 3 green onions, chopped

1 red onion, chopped
1 (10-ounce) package frozen peas,
  thawed
1 cup mayonnaise
1 cup mayonnaise-style salad
  dressing
4 cups shredded Swiss cheese

Layer the leaf lettuce, bacon, eggs, spinach, green onions, red onion and peas in a clear glass dish or bowl. Press gently to compact the layers. Combine the mayonnaise and mayonnaise-style salad dressing in a small bowl and mix well. Spread the mixture over the salad. Chill, covered, for 8 to 10 hours before serving. Sprinkle the Swiss cheese over the top immediately before serving.

Yield: 8 servings

Ramen Noodle Salad

2 (3-ounce) packages ramen noodles
  (any flavor), crumbled
1 (16-ounce) package coleslaw mix
2 bunches green onions, finely
  chopped
1 cup slivered almonds

1 cup sunflower seed kernels
3/4 cup (or less) vegetable oil
1/2 cup (or less) sugar
2 seasoning packets from ramen
  noodles
1/3 cup vinegar

Combine the ramen noodles, coleslaw mix, green onions, almonds and sunflower seed kernels in a salad bowl. Combine the oil, sugar, seasoning packets and vinegar in a bowl and mix until well blended. Pour over the salad and toss to mix well. Chill, covered, for 2 hours before serving.

Yield: 6 to 8 servings

Carolina Coleslaw

1 cup sugar
1 cup cider vinegar
2/3 cup vegetable oil
1 teaspoon salt
1 teaspoon dry mustard

1 teaspoon celery seeds
1 head cabbage, shredded
1 green bell pepper, thinly sliced
1 onion, thinly sliced

Combine the sugar, vinegar, oil, salt, dry mustard and celery seeds in a saucepan. Bring to a boil over medium-high heat and cook until the sugar dissolves, stirring frequently. Remove from the heat and refrigerate until chilled. Pour over the cabbage, bell pepper and onion in a large bowl; toss.

Yield: 8 to 10 servings

Boston Bean Salad

1 (15-ounce) can navy beans,
   rinsed, drained
1 (15-ounce) can small red beans,
   rinsed, drained
1 (15-ounce) can black beans,
   rinsed, drained
2 ribs celery, sliced
1/2 cup thinly sliced green onions

1/2 cup vinegar
1/4 cup molasses
1/4 cup salad oil
1 tablespoon Dijon mustard
1/4 teaspoon pepper
Lettuce leaves
2 cups torn curly endive
2 slices bacon, crisp-cooked, crumbled

Combine the navy beans, red beans, black beans, celery and green onions in a large bowl. Combine the vinegar, molasses, oil, mustard and pepper in a jar with a tight-fitting lid. Secure the lid and shake vigorously to mix well. Pour the dressing over the bean mixture and stir to coat well. Chill, covered, for 4 to 24 hours before serving, stirring frequently. To serve, line a salad bowl or platter with the lettuce leaves. Stir the curly endive and bacon into the bean salad. Spoon the bean salad into the prepared bowl with a slotted spoon. Garnish with green onions if desired.

Yield: 10 to 12 servings

Broccoli Salad

2 bunches broccoli, finely chopped
1/4 cup chopped red onion
8 slices bacon, crisp-cooked,
  crumbled
1 cup raisins
1 cup sunflower seed kernels

1/2 cup mayonnaise
3 tablespoons sugar
1 tablespoon wine
  vinegar

Combine the broccoli, onion, bacon, raisins and sunflower seed kernels in a bowl and mix well. Combine the mayonnaise, sugar and vinegar in a blender container and process until well blended and the sugar is dissolved. Pour the dressing over the broccoli mixture and toss to coat well.

Yield: 8 servings

Known as the "Father of Greenville," Vardry McBee purchased over 11,000 acres from Lemuel Alston in 1815. McBee donated the land for Greenville's first four churches.

Broccoli Cauliflower Salad

2 stalks broccoli, cut into
  small pieces
1 head cauliflower, cut into
  small pieces
1/2 cup sliced green onions
1 1/2 cups shredded Cheddar cheese
1 1/2 cups shredded mozzarella
  cheese

2 cups mayonnaise
1/4 cup sugar
1 tablespoon vinegar
1/2 teaspoon salt
1 pound bacon,
  crisp-cooked, crumbled

Combine the broccoli, cauliflower, green onions, Cheddar cheese and mozzarella cheese in a large bowl. Combine the mayonnaise, sugar, vinegar and salt in a bowl and mix until well blended. Pour the dressing over the broccoli mixture and toss to coat well. Fold in the bacon before serving.

Yield: 12 to 15 servings

Tomato and Eggplant Salad

3 pounds ripe tomatoes (assorted
    sizes)
2 (1-pound) eggplants, peeled,
    sliced into 1/2-inch rounds
3 tablespoons extra-virgin olive oil
3/4 teaspoon salt

1/4 teaspoon pepper
2 tablespoons red wine vinegar
11/2 teaspoons minced garlic
1/2 small shallot, minced
20 fresh basil leaves, rinsed, dried,
    10 leaves cut into ribbons

Cut the large tomatoes into wedges, the medium ones in half and leave the small tomatoes whole; set aside. Brush both sides of the eggplant rounds with the olive oil. Sprinkle with 1/4 teaspoon salt and 1/8 teaspoon pepper. Grill the eggplant over hot coals for 3 minutes per side. Arrange the tomatoes in the center of a serving platter. Arrange the grilled eggplant around the tomatoes. Combine 1/2 teaspoon salt, 1/8 teaspoon pepper, vinegar, garlic, shallot and the 10 basil leaves cut into ribbons in a bowl and mix well. Drizzle over the top of the tomatoes and eggplant. Garnish with the 10 whole basil leaves.

Yield: 15 servings

Italian Pasta Salad

4 ounces pepperoni, sliced into
    bite-size pieces
4 ounces hard salami, sliced into
    bite-size pieces
4 ounces provolone cheese, sliced
    into bite-size pieces
1 green bell pepper, finely chopped
1 onion, finely chopped

2 medium tomatoes, chopped
4 ounces each black and green olives
1 teaspoon oregano
1 teaspoon each salt and pepper
1 teaspoon garlic powder
1/3 cup vegetable oil
1/4 cup vinegar
1 pound rotini, cooked, drained

Combine the pepperoni, salami, cheese, bell pepper, onion, tomatoes, olives, oregano, salt, pepper, garlic powder, oil and vinegar in a salad bowl. Fold in the rotini and toss to coat well. Chill, covered, for 2 hours or more before serving.

Yield: 12 to 15 servings

Southern Potato Salad

3 pounds potatoes
1/2 cup chopped celery
1/4 cup finely chopped onion
2 hard-cooked eggs, chopped
1/2 cup mayonnaise

1/4 cup zesty Italian salad dressing
1 teaspoon salt
1/8 teaspoon pepper
Chopped fresh parsley (optional)

Cook the potatoes in boiling water in a large saucepan until tender; drain.
Let stand until cool and peel. Cut the potatoes into cubes. Combine the
potatoes, celery, onion and eggs in a large bowl. Stir in the mayonnaise, Italian
dressing, salt and pepper until well coated. Add the parsley.
Yield: 4 to 6 servings

German Potato Salad

8 ounces bacon
2 tablespoons flour
1/4 cup sugar
1/2 cup cider vinegar
1 cup water
2 tablespoons butter

1 cup sour cream
3 pounds potatoes
1 cup chopped onion
1 teaspoon salt
Pepper to taste

Fry the bacon in a skillet until crisp; reserve 1/4 cup bacon drippings.
Crumble the bacon and set aside. Heat the bacon drippings in a skillet. Stir in
the flour, sugar and vinegar. Add the water and butter. Bring to a boil and cook
until thickened. Remove from the heat and let cool. Stir in the sour cream.
Cook the potatoes in boiling water in a Dutch oven until tender; cool. Peel
and slice the potatoes. Combine the potatoes, crumbled bacon, onion, salt and
pepper in a large bowl. Pour the prepared dressing over the potatoes and stir to
coat well. Serve warm or chilled.
Yield: 4 to 6 servings

Greek Salad

Greek Dressing
1/4 cup olive oil
1/4 cup salad oil
3 tablespoons white wine vinegar
1/2 teaspoon salt
Freshly ground pepper to taste
1/8 teaspoon dry mustard
1 teaspoon parsley flakes

Salad
Lettuce, torn into bite-size pieces
Onion, cut into rings
Cucumber slices
Tomato wedges
Black olives, pitted
Feta cheese, crumbled
Greek peppers

　　For the dressing, combine the olive oil, salad oil, vinegar, salt, pepper, dry mustard and parsley in a blender and process until blended. Chill until serving time.
　　For the salad, toss all the ingredients in a large salad bowl. Pour the dressing over the top and toss to mix well. Serve immediately.
　　Yield: Variable

Oriental Chicken Salad

6 to 8 cups chopped cooked chicken
2 cups chopped celery
2 cups green grapes, sliced
1 to 2 cups toasted slivered
　　almonds
1 (8-ounce) can water chestnuts,
　　drained, sliced

2 cups mayonnaise
4 teaspoons soy sauce
Lemon juice to taste
2 teaspoons curry powder
Lettuce

　　Combine the chicken, celery, grapes, almonds and water chestnuts in a bowl. Stir in the mayonnaise, soy sauce, lemon juice and curry powder. Chill, covered, until serving time. Serve on beds of lettuce.
　　Yield 14 to 16 servings

Cranberry Salad

1 (3-ounce) package cherry gelatin
1 (3-ounce) package raspberry
   gelatin
3/4 cup sugar
3 cups boiling water
1 (12-ounce) package fresh
   cranberries, crushed

1 red apple, finely chopped
1 (8-ounce) can crushed
   pineapple, drained
1 cup chopped pecans
Whipped topping

Add the gelatin and sugar to the boiling water in a bowl, stirring until dissolved. Stir in the cranberries, apple, pineapple and pecans. Pour into a 9×13-inch dish. Chill until firm. Serve with whipped topping.

   Yield: 15 servings

 Founded in 1820 as St. James Mission, Christ Episcopal Church is the oldest congregation in Greenville and its church building, consecrated in 1853, is the oldest church structure. Christ Church is the mother church of Church of the Redeemer.

Fruit Salad

1 (4-ounce) package vanilla
   pudding
1 package tapioca
3 cups milk

1 tablespoon orange juice
1 cup mandarin oranges
1 cup chopped pineapple
2 bananas, sliced

Cook the pudding and tapioca with 3 cups milk in a saucepan according to the package directions. Remove from the heat and let cool. Stir in the orange juice, mandarin oranges, pineapple and bananas. Chill until serving time.

   Yield: 8 servings

Side Dishes

Braised Artichokes with Mushrooms and Onions

4 artichokes, stems trimmed
1 lemon, halved
Salt and pepper to taste
Juice of 1 lemon
1/4 cup olive oil
2 cups small white onions
2 carrots, sliced
1/4 pound mushrooms, sliced

2 garlic cloves, minced
1 1/2 cups chicken broth
1/2 cup dry white wine
1/3 cup white wine vinegar
Bouquet garni of 1 rib celery, white
    part of 1 small leek, 1 sprig fresh
    thyme and 1 bay leaf

Cut the top third off of each artichoke. Rub the cut edges with a lemon half. Snip off the points from all leaves. Scoop out the inedible chokes with a spoon and discard. Season the inside of each artichoke with juice of half the lemon, salt and pepper. Place the artichokes in a bowl of cold water. Add the juice of 1 lemon.

Heat the olive oil in a saucepan until hot. Add the onions and carrots. Cook for 5 minutes, stirring occasionally. Add the mushrooms, garlic, salt and pepper and cook for 3 minutes, stirring occasionally. Drain the artichokes and add to the saucepan, turning to coat with the oil. Add the broth, wine, vinegar and bouquet garni. Bring to a boil.

Reduce the heat and cover the saucepan with a round of buttered waxed paper and the saucepan lid. Braise over low heat for 30 to 40 minutes or until the artichokes are tender, basting with the liquid occasionally.

Yield: 4 servings

Oven-Roasted Green Beans

2 teaspoons olive oil
1 pound fresh green beans,
   trimmed

1 tablespoon butter, melted
Kosher or sea salt to taste

Brush a shallow baking pan with the olive oil. Arrange the green beans in a single layer in the pan. Roast at 450 degrees on the lowest rack of the oven for 10 to 12 minutes or until tender and just beginning to brown. Toss with the butter to coat. Sprinkle with the salt.
   Yield: 4 servings

Zesty Black-Eyed Peas

1 (16-ounce) package frozen
   black-eyed peas
1 1/4 cups chopped green bell
   pepper
3/4 cup chopped onion

3 tablespoons bacon drippings
1 (8-ounce) can diced
   tomatoes
Salt and pepper to taste

Cook the black-eyed peas using the package directions; drain. Sauté the bell pepper and onion in the bacon drippings in a skillet until tender. Add the black-eyed peas, undrained tomatoes, salt and pepper and cook over low heat until heated through, stirring frequently.
   Yield: 6 servings

Come Lord Jesus, be our holy guest, our morning joy, our evening rest, and with our daily bread impart your love and peace to every heart. Amen.

Asparagus with English Peas

1/4 cup (1/2 stick) butter
1/4 cup flour
2 cups milk
2 teaspoons onion juice
1 teaspoon Worcestershire sauce
1 (2-ounce) jar chopped pimentos
1/2 cup shredded Cheddar cheese
Salt and pepper to taste

1 (17-ounce) can asparagus, drained
1 (8-ounce) can sliced water
   chestnuts, drained
1 (17-ounce) can English peas,
   drained
1 (17-ounce) can artichoke hearts,
   drained
Buttered bread crumbs

Melt the butter in a medium saucepan over low heat. Stir in the flour. Add the milk gradually, stirring constantly. Cook until the mixture is thickened, stirring constantly. Stir in the onion juice, Worcestershire sauce, pimentos, Cheddar cheese, salt and pepper. Layer the asparagus, half of the white sauce, water chestnuts, peas and artichoke hearts in a buttered 2-quart baking dish. Pour the remaining white sauce over the top. Sprinkle with the bread crumbs. Bake at 350 degrees for 20 to 30 minutes or until heated through.

Yield: 10 servings

Corn Pudding

1 (17-ounce) can cream-style corn
1 (2-ounce) jar chopped pimentos,
   drained
2 eggs, slightly beaten
1 cup shredded medium-sharp
   Cheddar cheese

1/2 cup milk
2 tablespoons flour
2 tablespoons sugar
2 tablespoons margarine, melted

Combine the corn, pimentos, eggs, Cheddar cheese, milk, flour, sugar and margarine in a bowl and mix well. Pour the mixture into a greased 1 1/2-quart baking dish. Bake at 350 degrees for 45 to 50 minutes or until light brown.

Yield: 4 servings

Carrot and Cauliflower Bake

2 cups thinly sliced carrots
2 cups cauliflower florets
2 tablespoons butter
2 tablespoons flour
1 1/2 cups half-and-half
2 chicken-flavored bouillon cubes,
   crushed

1/2 teaspoon Dijon mustard
1/2 teaspoon dillweed
Dash of nutmeg
Dash of pepper
3/4 cup shredded Cheddar cheese
1 tablespoon butter, melted
1/4 cup bread crumbs

    Cook the carrots and cauliflower in a small amount of water in a saucepan for 10 minutes; drain. Melt 2 tablespoons butter in a saucepan. Stir in the flour. Cook over low heat just until mixture begins to brown, stirring constantly. Add the half-and-half gradually, stirring constantly. Stir in the bouillon cubes, Dijon mustard, dillweed, nutmeg and pepper. Cook until the mixture begins to boil, stirring constantly. Stir in the vegetable mixture. Spoon into a shallow 2- or 3-quart baking dish. Sprinkle with the Cheddar cheese. Combine 1 tablespoon butter and the bread crumbs and toss to mix. Sprinkle over the Cheddar cheese. Bake at 350 degrees for 20 to 25 minutes or until bubbly.
    Yield: 8 servings

Copper Pennies

1 pound carrots, sliced
1 small red bell pepper, finely
   chopped
1 onion, finely chopped
1 cup sugar

1/2 cup vegetable oil
1/4 cup vinegar
1 teaspoon dry mustard
1 teaspoon Worcestershire sauce
1 (10-ounce) can tomato soup

    Cook the carrots in a small amount of water in a saucepan until tender; drain. Combine the carrots, bell pepper and onion in a bowl and toss to mix. Combine the sugar, oil, vinegar, dry mustard, Worcestershire sauce and tomato soup in a saucepan and bring to a boil, stirring frequently. Pour the tomato soup mixture over the vegetables. Chill, covered, for 8 hours. This will keep for up to 2 weeks.
    Yield: 6 to 8 servings

Braised Fennel with Parmesan

4 fennel bulbs, trimmed
Salt to taste
1/3 cup butter

Freshly ground pepper to taste
1/3 cup freshly grated Parmesan
cheese

Peel and discard the outer layer of the fennel bulbs. Chop the fennel bulbs into medium wedges. Combine the fennel with enough boiling salted water to cover in a saucepan. Boil for 5 minutes; drain. Melt the butter in a skillet. Add the fennel. Sprinkle with salt and pepper. Sauté over medium heat for 5 to 8 minutes or until tender. Arrange in a serving dish and sprinkle with the Parmesan cheese.

Yield: 4 servings

Goat Cheese Mashed Potato Gratin

2 pounds Yukon Gold or russet
    potatoes, peeled, chopped
6 garlic cloves
Salt to taste
1/2 cup (1 stick) butter

1/3 cup heavy cream
1/3 cup soft mild goat cheese
Pepper to taste
1/4 cup finely chopped green
    onions

Combine the potatoes, unpeeled garlic and salt to taste with enough water to cover in a saucepan. Simmer, covered, for 15 to 25 minutes or until potatoes are tender; drain. Combine the butter, cream, goat cheese, salt and pepper to taste in a saucepan. Cook over low heat until the butter and cheese are melted and mixture is blended, stirring frequently. Press the potatoes and garlic through a food mill or ricer into a bowl. Add the goat cheese mixture, salt and pepper and beat until fluffy. Do not overbeat. Stir in the green onions. Spoon into a shallow 1-quart baking dish. Broil for 3 to 5 minutes or until golden. You may prepare the potatoes and keep chilled, covered, up to 2 days in advance. Bake the potatoes at 400 degrees for 20 minutes or until heated through before broiling.

Yield: 4 to 6 servings

Potato and Spinach Galette

3 tablespoons virgin olive oil
1 tablespoon butter
1 1/2 to 2 pounds potatoes, peeled,
   thinly sliced
1/4 teaspoon seasoned salt
1 tablespoon butter
1 tablespoon virgin olive oil
1 1/2 tablespoons chopped garlic

1 pound fresh spinach,
   stems removed
1/4 teaspoon seasoned
   salt
1/4 teaspoon pepper
1 tablespoon virgin
   olive oil

Heat 3 tablespoons olive oil and 1 tablespoon butter in an
ovenproof skillet. Add the potatoes and toss to coat. Sprinkle
with 1/4 teaspoon seasoned salt. Sauté over high heat until
tender. Remove the potatoes to a plate. Heat 1 tablespoon
butter and 1 tablespoon olive oil. Add the garlic and sauté for
10 seconds. Add the spinach, 1/4 teaspoon seasoned salt and
pepper. Sauté until the spinach is wilted and most of the liquid
has evaporated. Remove the spinach to a plate.

Coat the skillet with 1 tablespoon olive oil. Arrange 1/4 of
the potatoes over the bottom and 1/2 inch up the side of the
skillet. Layer 1/4 of the potatoes over the prepared layer.
Spoon the spinach over the potatoes. Arrange the remaining
potatoes over the spinach. You may prepare the recipe up to
this point and let stand, covered, for up to 6 hours.

Bake at 400 degrees for 30 minutes. Remove the skillet
from the oven and cook on the stovetop over medium-high
heat to brown the bottom layer, shaking the skillet to keep the
potatoes from sticking.

To serve, invert the galette onto a serving platter and cut
into wedges.

Yield: 4 servings

 Greenville
landmarks, the
Poinsett Hotel,
Poinsett Club, and
Poinsett Highway
were all named for
America's ambassador
to Mexico and world
traveler, Joel Roberts
Poinsett (1779–1851).
In 1820, Poinsett,
U.S. ambassador to
Mexico, brought the
beautiful Mexican
flower (now known
as the Poinsettia) to
Greenville and
domesticated it in
South Carolina.

Onion Pie

1 cup crushed crackers
1/4 cup (1/2 stick) melted
    margarine
2 cups sliced onions
1 tablespoon margarine
2 eggs, beaten

1/4 cup milk
Salt and pepper to taste
1 cup shredded sharp Cheddar
    cheese
Paprika

Combine the crushed crackers and 1/4 cup margarine in a bowl and mix well. Press over the bottom and up the side of a 9-inch pie plate. Sauté the onions in 1 tablespoon margarine in a skillet until transparent. Spoon the onions into the prepared pie plate. Combine the eggs, milk, salt and pepper in a bowl and mix well. Pour over the onions. Sprinkle with the cheese and paprika. Bake at 350 degrees for 30 minutes.

Yield: 6 to 8 servings

Sweet Potato Soufflé

3 cups mashed cooked sweet
    potatoes
1 cup sugar
1/2 cup (1 stick) butter or
    margarine, melted
2 eggs, beaten

1 teaspoon vanilla extract
2 cups pecan halves
1 cup packed brown sugar
1/3 cup flour
1/3 cup butter, melted

Combine the sweet potatoes, sugar, 1/2 cup butter, eggs and vanilla in a bowl and mix well. Spoon into an oblong baking dish. Toss the pecans, brown sugar and flour in a bowl. Sprinkle over the sweet potatoes. Drizzle with the 1/3 cup melted butter. Bake at 300 degrees for 30 minutes. You may substitute 1 cup pecan halves and 1 cup flaked coconut for the 2 cups pecan halves if desired.

Yield: 6 servings

Summer Squash Casserole

4 yellow squash, sliced
1 onion, finely chopped
1 cup shredded Cheddar cheese
1/2 cup mayonnaise
1 egg

Cayenne pepper (optional)
Oregano (optional)
Salt and black pepper (optional)
12 butter crackers, crushed

Combine the squash and onion with enough water to cover in a saucepan. Cook until tender; drain. Add the cheese, mayonnaise, egg, cayenne, oregano, salt and black pepper and stir gently to mix. Spoon into a baking dish. Sprinkle with the cracker crumbs. Bake at 350 degrees for 30 minutes.

Yield: 4 servings

Fresh Tomato Pie

2 to 3 large very ripe tomatoes,
  peeled, sliced
Salt to taste
2 to 3 green onions, chopped
Pepper to taste
1/2 cup chopped fresh basil

2 tablespoons chopped fresh chives
1 baked (9-inch) pie shell
1 cup shredded sharp Cheddar
  cheese
1 cup mayonnaise

Sprinkle the tomatoes with salt. Let drain on a rack for 15 to 30 minutes. Pat dry with a paper towel. Layer the tomatoes, green onions, salt, pepper, basil and chives 1/2 at a time in the prepared pie shell. Combine the cheese and mayonnaise in a bowl and mix well. Spread over the prepared layers. Bake at 350 degrees for 30 minutes or until light brown.

Yield: 6 servings

Apples and Cranberries

3 cups chopped peeled apples
2 cups fresh cranberries
1/4 cup sugar
1/2 cup quick-cooking oats

1/2 cup packed brown sugar
1/2 cup chopped pecans
1/2 cup (1 stick) butter, melted
1/3 cup flour

Mix the apples, cranberries and sugar in a bowl. Spoon into a 2-quart baking dish. Combine the oats, brown sugar, pecans, melted butter and flour in a bowl and mix until crumbly. Spoon the oat mixture over the top. Bake at 350 degrees for 1 hour. Serve warm or cold.

Yield: 12 servings

Hot Fruit Bake

1 (20-ounce) can sliced pineapple
1 (17-ounce) can apricot halves
1 (16-ounce) can peach halves
1 (16-ounce) can pear halves
1 (14 1/2-ounce) jar sliced spiced
   apple rings

1/2 cup (1 stick) butter or
   margarine
1/2 cup sugar
1 tablespoon cornstarch
1 cup dry sherry

Drain the fruit, discarding the juice. Combine the drained fruit in a 2-quart baking dish. Melt the butter in a saucepan over medium heat. Combine the sugar and cornstarch in a small bowl. Add to the melted butter. Cook until slightly thickened, stirring constantly. Stir in the sherry. Pour over the fruit. Bake at 350 degrees for 35 to 40 minutes or until bubbly.

Yield: 8 servings

Champagne Rice Pilaf

1 1/3 sticks butter
2 cups long-grain white rice
1 1/3 cups vermicelli
2 2/3 cups chicken broth

1 1/3 cups Champagne
Pinch of salt
1/2 cup slivered
    blanched almonds

    Melt the butter in a saucepan. Add the rice and vermicelli. Sauté for 7 to 10 minutes or until the rice is golden brown and makes a popping sound. Combine the chicken broth and Champagne in a saucepan. Bring to a boil, stirring occasionally. Pour the Champagne mixture over the rice mixture. Stir in the salt. Spoon the mixture into a baking dish. Bake at 350 degrees for 45 to 60 minutes or until all of the liquid is absorbed. Sprinkle with the almonds. You may substitute sliced water chestnuts for the almonds and white wine for the Champagne if desired.
    Yield: 8 servings

The Greenville Little Theater launched the acting career of Greenville native and Academy Award winner Joanne Woodward, whose films include *The Three Faces of Eve* (1957) and *The Glass Menagerie* (1987), which was directed by her husband, Paul Newman.

Spanish Rice

6 slices bacon
1/4 cup chopped green bell pepper
1/4 cup chopped onion

3 cups cooked rice
1 (15-ounce) can tomatoes
Salt and pepper to taste

    Fry the bacon in a skillet until crisp; remove and crumble. Drain, reserving 2 tablespoons of the bacon drippings. Stir the bell pepper and onion into the reserved drippings. Cook until the onion is tender, stirring frequently. Stir in the bacon, rice, tomatoes and salt and pepper. Cook over low heat for 15 minutes or until heated through, stirring occasionally.
    Yield: 6 servings

Veggie Wild Rice

1 (14-ounce) can vegetable broth
3/4 cup water
1 (6-ounce) package long grain and
    wild rice mix
3 tablespoons chopped walnuts
1 cup sliced mushrooms

1/2 medium red bell pepper,
    chopped
1 garlic clove, minced
3 green onions, sliced
1/2 teaspoon salt
1/2 teaspoon freshly ground pepper

Bring the vegetable broth and water to a boil in a medium saucepan. Add the wild rice mix, discarding the seasoning packet. Reduce the heat and simmer, covered, for 30 minutes. Sauté the walnuts in a large nonstick skillet coated with nonstick cooking spray over medium high heat for 5 minutes. Remove the walnuts to a plate.

Sauté the mushrooms, bell pepper and garlic in the skillet over medium-high heat for 5 minutes or until the vegetables are tender. Stir in the cooked rice, green onions, salt and pepper. Sprinkle with the toasted walnuts. Serve immediately.

Yield: 8 servings

Old South Corn Bread Dressing

1/4 cup vegetable oil
2 cups self-rising cornmeal
1 cup milk
1 egg
6 cups soft bread cubes
2 teaspoons sage
1 teaspoon thyme
1/2 teaspoon salt

1/8 teaspoon pepper
6 slices bacon, cut into 3/4-inch
  pieces
2 cups chopped celery
1 cup chopped green onions
11/2 cups chicken broth
3 eggs, hard-cooked, chopped
1/4 cup (1/2 stick) butter, melted

Pour the oil into a cast-iron skillet. Place the skillet in the oven. Heat the oven to 400 degrees. Combine the cornmeal and milk in a bowl and mix well. Beat in the egg. Pour the hot oil into the cornmeal mixture and stir until blended. Pour the cornmeal mixture into the skillet. Bake at 400 degrees for 20 minutes. Cool slightly.

Crumble the corn bread into a bowl. Add the bread cubes, sage, thyme, salt and pepper and toss to mix. Fry the bacon in a skillet until crisp. Remove the bacon to paper towels using a slotted spoon, reserving the drippings. Crumble the bacon. Cook the celery and green onions in the reserved drippings until tender. Add to the corn bread mixture and stir gently to mix. Add the chicken broth and mix well. Stir in the crumbled bacon, eggs and butter. Spoon into a 3-quart casserole. Bake, loosely covered, at 350 degrees for 1 hour.

Yield: 12 servings

Pasta & Vegetarian

Pasta with Asparagus

1/4 cup olive oil
1 tablespoon butter
1 garlic clove, minced
1 teaspoon red pepper flakes
2 to 3 dashes hot red pepper sauce
1 pound fresh asparagus, trimmed,
   cut into 2-inch pieces

1/4 teaspoon salt
1/4 teaspoon black pepper
1/4 cup grated Parmesan cheese
8 ounces shell pasta, cooked,
   drained

    Heat the olive oil and butter in a large skillet. Add the garlic, pepper flakes and hot pepper sauce and sauté for 2 to 3 minutes. Add the asparagus, salt and black pepper and sauté for 8 to 10 minutes or until the asparagus is tender-crisp. Stir in the Parmesan cheese and cook until melted. Place the pasta in a large bowl. Top with the sauce and toss to coat. Serve immediately.
    Yield: 4 servings

Thirty-Minute Pomodoro Sauce (Tony Danza)

2 large cans Progresso Plum
   Tomatoes with Basil
Salt and pepper to taste
Freshly grated Parmesan cheese
   to taste

Chopped fresh basil to taste
Wine to taste
1/4 cup olive oil
10 garlic cloves, coarsely chopped
1 (6-ounce) can tomato paste

    Strain the tomatoes through a colander over a large saucepan. Press with a spoon to remove the juice. Discard the pulp. Season the tomato juice with a little salt and a lot of pepper. Stir in Parmesan cheese, basil and wine. Heat the olive oil in a small saucepan. Add the garlic and sauté until lightly browned. Stir in the tomato paste. Cook until the garlic is softened. Add to the tomato basil mixture and stir to mix. Simmer over low heat for 20 minutes. Serve over your favorite pasta.
    Yield: 6 servings

Mrs. Fusco's Pasta with Broccoli (Tim Conway)

Florets of 1/2 bunch broccoli
Florets of 1/2 head cauliflower
3 small zucchini, sliced
Salt to taste
1/4 cup olive oil
4 garlic cloves, chopped

Pepper to taste
16 ounces penne pasta (or your favorite pasta), cooked al dente, drained
3 tablespoons chopped fresh basil
Freshly grated Parmesan cheese

Cook the broccoli, cauliflower and zucchini in lightly salted boiling water until tender-crisp; drain. Heat the olive oil in a large skillet or wok. Add the garlic and sauté slowly for a few minutes, being careful not to burn. Add the vegetables and toss to coat. Season with salt and pepper. Cook, while tossing, until the vegetables are heated through. Place the hot pasta in a large bowl. Top with the vegetables and basil. Toss to coat. Top with Parmesan cheese.

Yield: 8 servings

Mediterranean Pasta

2 tablespoons olive oil
1 large garlic clove, minced
2 tablespoons chopped shallots
2 tablespoons white wine
4 ounces feta cheese
1 (14-ounce) can artichoke hearts, drained, chopped

1 (14-ounce) can tomatoes
1/4 cup sliced black olives
4 ounces sliced mushrooms
8 ounces linguini, cooked, drained
4 ounces grated Asiago cheese
Capers

Heat the olive oil in a large saucepan. Add the garlic, shallots and wine and sauté until softened. Stir in the feta cheese. Cook, stirring constantly, until the cheese melts. Stir in the artichoke hearts, tomatoes, olives and mushrooms. Cook, stirring constantly, just until heated through. Serve over the hot linguini and top with the Asiago cheese and capers.

Yield: 6 servings

Manicotti

8 ounces ground beef
1 garlic clove, minced
1 cup cottage cheese
1/2 teaspoon salt
1/2 cup mayonnaise

8 manicotti shells, cooked, drained
1 (16-ounce) jar spaghetti sauce
1/2 teaspoon dried oregano leaves
Grated Parmesan cheese

Brown the ground beef and garlic in a skillet, drain. Mix the cottage cheese, salt and mayonnaise in a bowl. Stir in the ground beef. Fill each manicotti shell with about 1/4 cup of filling. Arrange the filled shells in a single layer in a baking dish. Sprinkle any remaining filling over the top. Cover with the spaghetti sauce and sprinkle with the oregano and Parmesan cheese. Cover with foil. Bake at 325 degrees for 15 minutes. Remove the foil and bake for 10 minutes.

Yield: 4 servings

Creamy Chicken Manicotti

1 (10-ounce) can cream of chicken
  or cream of mushroom soup
1 cup sour cream
2 cups cooked cubed chicken
2 tablespoons margarine
2 tablespoons chopped onion

1 (2 1/2-ounce) jar sliced
  mushrooms
8 manicotti shells, cooked, drained
1 cup shredded Monterey Jack
  cheese

Mix the soup and sour cream in a bowl. Remove half to another bowl and stir in the chicken. Melt the margarine in a small saucepan. Add the onion and sauté until softened. Stir in the undrained mushrooms. Add the mushroom mixture to the soup and sour cream mixture. Stir to mix. Fill the manicotti shells with the chicken mixture. Arrange the filled shells in a single layer in a baking dish. Spoon the onion mixture over the top. Bake at 350 degrees for 15 to 20 minutes or until heated through. Top with the Monterey Jack cheese and bake for 5 minutes.

Yield: 4 servings

Hoopla Chicken Lasagna

2 tablespoons butter or margarine
1 cup chopped onion
2 garlic cloves, minced
2 (26-ounce) jars spaghetti sauce
  (any flavor)
1/2 cup water
1 (4-ounce) can chopped green
  chiles, drained
1 teaspoon cumin
8 ounces cream cheese, softened

2 teaspoons chicken bouillon
  granules
3 cups cooked chopped chicken
4 cups shredded mozzarella
  cheese
3/4 cup chopped celery
16 ounces lasagna noodles,
  cooked, drained

Melt the butter in a large heavy saucepan over medium heat. Add the onion and garlic and sauté until softened. Stir in the spaghetti sauce, water, chiles and cumin. Bring to a boil, reduce the heat and simmer for 10 minutes.

Beat the cream cheese and bouillon in a mixing bowl until fluffy. Stir in the chicken, 1 cup of the mozzarella cheese and the celery. Spread 3/4 cup of the sauce mixture in the bottom of a greased 9×15-inch baking dish. Top with half the lasagna noodles, half the chicken mixture and 1 1/2 cups of mozzarella cheese. Top with half the remaining sauce and the remaining chicken mixture. Top with the remaining sauce.

Cover and bake at 375 degrees for 45 minutes or until hot and bubbly. Uncover and sprinkle with the remaining 1 1/2 cups mozzarella cheese. Bake for 5 minutes.

Yield: 12 to 15 servings

Father, thank you for allowing us to share this meal together. Send your Spirit to bless these gifts which you give us to sustain our lives. We thank you for them, and for ALL your blessings, in the name of your Son, Jesus Christ. Amen.

Shrimp and Artichoke Fettuccini

4 to 5 teaspoons olive oil
2 to 3 garlic cloves, minced
1 teaspoon red pepper flakes
1 to 1 1/2 pounds shrimp, peeled, deveined
3 to 4 green onions, chopped
1 (14-ounce) can artichoke hearts, drained, quartered
2 tablespoons (or more) heavy cream or half-and-half
2 tablespoons prepared pesto
8 ounces fettuccini, cooked, drained
Freshly grated Parmesan cheese for garnish
Chopped fresh parsley for garnish

Heat the olive oil in a large skillet or wok. Add the garlic, pepper flakes and shrimp and stir-fry until the shrimp turn pink. Add the green onions, artichokes, cream and pesto. Stir to mix well. Add the fettuccini and cook, stirring often, until heated through. Add more cream if desired. Garnish with Parmesan cheese and parsley.

Yield: 4 to 5 servings

Penne with Shrimp and Bacon

4 ounces bacon, cut into narrow strips
1/2 cup frozen peas, thawed
8 ounces shrimp, peeled, halved, if large
1 1/2 tablespoons butter
1/2 cup ricotta cheese
1 tablespoon grated Parmesan cheese
Salt and pepper to taste
16 ounces penne rigate pasta

Sauté the bacon in a large skillet until partially cooked. Add the peas and sauté for 2 minutes. Stir in the shrimp and sauté until the shrimp turn pink. Add the butter and reduce the heat to very low. Mix the ricotta cheese and Parmesan cheese in a large bowl. Season with salt and pepper. Cook the pasta in a large saucepan of boiling salted water until al dente. Remove 2 to 3 tablespoons of cooking water from the pasta and whisk into the cheese mixture. Drain the pasta and add to the cheese. Toss to coat. Add the shrimp mixture and toss well.

Yield: 4 servings

Baked Spaghetti

2 slices bacon, chopped
2 onions, chopped
1 garlic clove, minced
12 ounces ground beef
1 1/2 teaspoons salt
1 teaspoon chili powder

2 (8-ounce) cans tomato sauce
2 1/2 cups water
Pepper to taste
1/2 cup sliced black olives
8 ounces uncooked spaghetti
1 cup shredded Cheddar cheese

Fry the bacon, onions and garlic in a large saucepan until the vegetables soften. Add the beef and cook, stirring, until no longer pink. Stir in the salt, chili powder, tomato sauce and water. Season with pepper. Cover and simmer for 25 minutes. Stir in the olives. Break half the spaghetti into a greased 2-quart baking dish. Cover with half the meat sauce. Top with half the cheese. Repeat the layers. Bake, covered, at 350 degrees for 30 minutes. Uncover and bake for 15 minutes.

Yield: 6 servings

Spinach and Spaghetti

1 egg, beaten
1/2 cup sour cream
1/4 cup milk
2 teaspoons instant minced onion
2 tablespoons grated Parmesan
  cheese
1/2 teaspoon salt
Dash of pepper

2 cups shredded Monterey Jack
  cheese
1 (10-ounce) package frozen
  chopped spinach, thawed,
  squeezed dry
4 ounces spaghetti, cooked, drained
Grated Parmesan cheese

Mix the egg, sour cream, milk, onion, 2 tablespoons Parmesan cheese, salt and pepper in a large bowl. Stir in the Monterey Jack cheese. Add the spinach and spaghetti and stir to mix well. Spoon into a greased baking dish. Sprinkle with Parmesan cheese. Bake, covered, at 350 degrees for 15 minutes. Uncover and bake for 20 minutes.

Yield: 4 servings

Spinach and Cheese Calzones

1/2 onion, chopped
1/2 to 3/4 (10-ounce) package
    frozen chopped spinach, thawed,
    well drained
Italian seasoning, salt and pepper
    to taste
1 (10-ounce) can refrigerated pizza
    dough

1/2 to 3/4 cup part-skim ricotta
    cheese
1/4 to 1/2 cup part-skim shredded
    mozzarella cheese
Marinara sauce (optional)

Sauté the onion in a skillet coated with nonstick cooking spray until softened. Remove from the heat and stir in the spinach. Season with Italian seasoning, salt and pepper. Stir to mix.

Unroll the pizza dough on a floured work surface. Pat or roll the dough about 3 inches larger in width and length. Cut into 4 rectangles. Place 1/4 of the ricotta cheese, 1/4 of the spinach mixture and 1/4 of the mozzarella cheese on each rectangle. Fold the dough over and crimp the edges to seal. Arrange on a greased baking sheet.

Bake at 425 degrees for 11 to 15 minutes or until golden brown. Serve warm with marinara sauce if desired.

Note: Feel free to vary the amounts of the filling ingredients or to change the fillings to include ingredients such as mushrooms, pepperoni, ham, bacon or Parmesan cheese.

Yield: 4 servings

Baked Eggplant

1 egg
1/4 cup milk
1 cup bread crumbs
6 tablespoons olive oil
1 (1 1/4-pound) eggplant, cut into
    12 (1/8-inch) slices
Salt and pepper to taste
1 cup ricotta cheese
1/4 teaspoon oregano

2 cups shredded
    Monterey Jack cheese
1 (15-ounce) can
    tomato sauce
1 cup water
2 teaspoons sugar
1/4 teaspoon pepper
1/4 teaspoon oregano

Mix the egg and milk in a shallow dish. Spread the bread crumbs on waxed paper. Brush half the olive oil on a 10×15-inch baking pan. Season the eggplant slices with salt and pepper. Dip half the eggplant slices in the egg mixture and then coat in the bread crumbs. Arrange in a single layer in the baking pan. Broil for 5 to 7 minutes, turning once, or until tender and lightly browned on both sides. Remove to a plate. Repeat with the remaining olive oil and eggplant.

Mix the ricotta cheese, 1/4 teaspoon oregano and all but 2 tablespoons of the Monterey Jack cheese in a bowl. Spoon about 2 tablespoons of this mixture in a 1/2-inch-wide strip on each eggplant slice. Roll up as for a jelly roll. Stir the tomato sauce, 1 cup water, sugar, 1/4 teaspoon pepper and 1/4 teaspoon oregano in a bowl. Spread some in the bottom of a 2-quart baking dish. Arrange the eggplant rolls, seam side down, on top of the sauce. Top with the remaining tomato sauce.

Bake at 350 degrees for 30 minutes or until heated through. Sprinkle with the remaining 2 tablespoons Monterey Jack cheese. Bake for 2 to 3 minutes.

Yield: 6 main-course servings or 12 first-course servings

Entrées

Special Occasion Filet Mignon

1 large or 2 medium tomatoes
1 teaspoon butter
2 tablespoons butter
1 large onion, cut into 1/2-inch
  slices

4 ounces mushrooms, fluted
4 (1-inch-thick) tenderloin steaks
1/2 cup water
2 tablespoons Dijon mustard
4 teaspoons capers, drained

Cut 4 thick center slices from the tomato. Melt 1 teaspoon butter in a 10-inch skillet over medium heat. Add the tomato slices and cook until heated through. Remove to a warm platter. Heat 2 tablespoons butter in a 12-inch skillet over medium heat. Add the sliced onion and cook until softened, stirring occasionally. Remove with a slotted spoon to a bowl. Heat the drippings over medium-high heat. Add the mushrooms and steaks and cook for 5 minutes, for medium-rare, turning the steaks once. Place one steak on each tomato slice and scatter the mushrooms on the platter. Keep warm. Add the water, mustard and capers to the drippings in the pan. Cook over medium heat, stirring constantly, until the mixture boils and thickens slightly. Add the onion and cook until heated through. Pour the sauce over and around the steaks.

Yield: 4 servings

London Broil on the Grill

1/2 cup red cooking wine
1/3 cup vegetable or olive oil
1/4 cup finely chopped onion
1 garlic clove, minced

1/2 teaspoon salt
1/2 teaspoon pepper
1 (2-pound) London Broil

Mix the wine, oil, onion, garlic, salt and pepper in a bowl. Place the London broil and marinade in a sealable plastic bag. Chill for 6 to 8 hours or overnight, turning the bag occasionally. Remove the London broil to a preheated grill at high heat. Grill for 35 to 40 minutes, or to desired doneness, turning every 10 to 15 minutes. Baste occasionally with the marinade during the first 20 minutes.

Yield: 8 servings

New England Boiled Dinner

1 (3-pound) boneless chuck roast
2 (10³/4-ounce) cans onion soup
2 tablespoons prepared horseradish
1 bay leaf
1 garlic clove, minced
1 pound rutabagas, cut into
    1/4-inch slices

6 carrots
8 small whole potatoes
1 medium head cabbage, cored,
    cut into 6 wedges
1/2 cup water
1/2 cup flour

Place the roast in a large heavy saucepan. Add the soup, horseradish, bay leaf and garlic. Cover and cook over low heat for 2 hours. Add the rutabagas, carrots, potatoes and cabbage. Cook for 30 minutes or until the vegetables are tender. Remove the meat and vegetables to a serving platter and keep warm; discard the bay leaf. Whisk the water and flour in a small bowl. Add to the saucepan. Cook, stirring constantly, until thickened. Serve with the meat and vegetables.

Yield: 8 servings

Beef Bourguignonne

2 tablespoons vegetable oil
5 onions, sliced
8 ounces mushrooms, sliced
2 pounds stew beef
1/4 teaspoon marjoram

1/4 teaspoon thyme
Salt and pepper to taste
1¹/2 tablespoons flour
3/4 cup beef broth
1¹/2 cups red wine

Heat the oil in a skillet. Add the onions and mushrooms and sauté until softened. Remove to a bowl and drain the skillet. Add the beef to the skillet and brown the beef. Sprinkle with the seasonings. Whisk the flour and broth in a small bowl. Add to the skillet. Heat to boiling, stirring constantly. Boil for 1 minute, stirring constantly. Stir in the wine and reduce the heat. Cover and simmer for 2¹/2 hours or until tender. Stir in the onions and mushrooms gently. Cook, uncovered, for 15 minutes or until heated through. Serve over rice.

Yield: 6 servings

Beef Stroganoff

1 tablespoon flour
1/2 teaspoon salt
1 pound round steak, cut into
    1-inch strips
2 tablespoons butter
1 cup thinly sliced mushrooms
1/2 cup chopped onion
1 garlic clove, minced

2 tablespoons butter
3 tablespoons flour
1 tablespoon tomato paste
1 (10 3/4-ounce) can beef stock,
    chilled
1 cup sour cream
2 tablespoons cooking sherry
Hot cooked rice or noodles

Mix 1 tablespoon flour and the salt in a shallow dish. Dredge the beef strips in the flour mixture. Melt 2 tablespoons butter in a skillet. Add the beef and brown quickly on all sides. Add the mushrooms, onion and garlic and sauté for 3 to 4 minutes or until the onion is barely softened. Remove to a bowl. Melt 2 tablespoons butter in the skillet. Stir in 3 tablespoons flour and the tomato paste. Add the beef stock slowly. Simmer until the mixture thickens. Stir in the beef and vegetables, sour cream and sherry. Cook over low heat until heated through, stirring often. Do not boil. Serve over rice or noodles.

Yield: 4 servings

Grilled Flank Steak

1 flank steak
Bottled Italian dressing
1/4 cup (1/2 stick) margarine,
    softened

Crumbled bleu cheese, softened

Place the flank steak in a sealable plastic bag. Add Italian dressing to cover. Seal the bag and chill for several hours. Remove the flank steak to a preheated grill. Grill for 7 minutes on one side and 5 minutes on the other side. Mix the margarine and bleu cheese in a bowl until blended. Smother the hot flank steak with the bleu cheese mixture before serving.

Yield: 4 to 8 servings

Chinese Pepper Steak

1 1/2 tablespoons soy sauce
2 teaspoons cornstarch
1 tablespoon wine
1 tablespoon sesame oil
1 teaspoon grated fresh gingerroot
1 garlic clove, minced
8 ounces thinly sliced round steak
3 tablespoons vegetable oil
1 cup sliced water chestnuts

1 cup thinly sliced green
  bell pepper
1/4 teaspoon salt
Pepper to taste
3 tablespoons vegetable oil
1 teaspoon cornstarch
2 teaspoons soy sauce
1/3 cup water
Hot cooked rice

Mix 1 1/2 tablespoon soy sauce, 2 teaspoons cornstarch, wine, sesame oil, gingerroot and garlic in a bowl. Place the round steak in a sealable plastic bag. Pour the marinade over the steak and seal the bag. Chill for 1 to 3 hours.

Heat 3 tablespoons vegetable oil in a large skillet over high heat. Add the water chestnuts, bell pepper and salt. Season with pepper. Sauté for 2 minutes. Remove to a platter. Add 3 tablespoons vegetable oil to the skillet and heat over high heat. Add the beef and marinade. Sauté for 2 to 3 minutes for medium-rare. Add the vegetables to the skillet.

Whisk the 1 teaspoon cornstarch, 2 teaspoons soy sauce and 1/3 cup water in a small bowl. Add to the skillet. Cook, stirring constantly, until the sauce thickens. Serve over rice.

Yield: 2 to 4 servings

Come, Lord Jesus, be our guest, and let these gifts to us be blessed. O give thanks unto the Lord for He is good, and His mercy endures forever. Amen.

Bleu Cheese Meat Loaf

12 ounces whole button
   mushrooms
1 1/2 pounds ground chuck

1/2 teaspoon garlic powder
1/4 teaspoon pepper
8 ounces bleu cheese, crumbled

    Select 6 or 7 mushrooms and remove the stems and set the caps aside. Chop the remaining mushrooms. Sauté the chopped mushrooms in a skillet coated with nonstick cooking spray. Drain well. Mix the beef, garlic powder and pepper in a bowl. Shape half the meat mixture into a round disk. Place in a baking dish and make a depression in the center. Fill with the bleu cheese and sautéed mushrooms. Shape the remaining meat mixture into a round disk and place on top. Pinch the edges of the meat together to seal. Arrange the mushroom caps in a decorative pattern on top of the meat. Push them gently into the meat so that they are partially imbedded. Bake at 350 degrees for 45 minutes or until cooked through. Drain the drippings after 30 minutes of baking.
    Yield: 4 servings

Easy Italian Meatballs

1 1/4 pounds ground beef
1/2 cup freshly grated Parmesan
   cheese
1 cup plain bread crumbs
1 garlic clove, minced
1 tablespoon chopped fresh parsley

1/2 cup milk
2 eggs, beaten
1 teaspoon Italian seasoning
1 teaspoon salt
1/4 teaspoon pepper
Extra-light olive oil for frying

    Combine the ground beef, Parmesan cheese, bread crumbs, garlic, parsley, milk, eggs, Italian seasoning, salt and pepper in a bowl. Mix well. Form gently into balls. Cover the bottom of a large skillet sparingly with olive oil. Heat over low to medium heat. Add the meatballs and cook until browned and cooked though. Drain on paper towels. Note: Simmer in your favorite pasta sauce for at least 30 minutes if desired, before serving.
    Yield: 6 servings

Family Favorite Macaroni and Beef Casserole

1 1/2 tablespoons butter
3/4 cup chopped onion
1/4 to 1/2 cup finely chopped green
    bell pepper
1 pound lean ground beef
2 teaspoons basil
1 to 2 teaspoons oregano
2 cups crushed tomatoes
1 teaspoon red wine vinegar
1 teaspoon sugar
Salt and black pepper to taste
2 tablespoons butter

2 tablespoons flour
2 cups milk
2 cups shredded Cheddar
    cheese
1/4 teaspoon nutmeg
Dash of cayenne pepper
8 ounces elbow macaroni,
    cooked al dente,
    drained
Freshly grated Parmesan
    cheese

Greenville is the home of the Greenville Braves, a Class "AA" affiliate of the Atlanta Braves. Other professional sports teams in Greenville include the Greenville Growwl hockey team and the Carolina Rhinos arena football team.

Melt 1 1/2 tablespoons butter in a large skillet. Add the onion and bell pepper and sauté until softened. Add the ground beef and cook until no longer pink. Drain off the fat. Stir in the basil, oregano, tomatoes, vinegar and sugar. Cook for 5 minutes. Season with salt and black pepper.

Melt 2 tablespoons butter in a medium saucepan. Stir in the flour. Stir in the milk and cook, stirring constantly, for 5 minutes or until smooth and thickened. Add the cheese and cook, stirring often, until the cheese melts. Stir in the nutmeg and cayenne pepper.

Place the macaroni in a buttered baking dish. Spoon the ground beef mixture over the macaroni. Top with the cheese sauce. Sprinkle with Parmesan cheese. Bake at 350 degrees for 25 minutes.

Yield: 6 servings

Apricot Pork Roast

2 tablespoons butter
3 pork tenderloins
Salt and pepper to taste
3/4 cup apricot jam

2 tablespoons butter
1 cup brown sauce with mushrooms
Chopped fresh parsley

   Melt 2 tablespoons butter in a Dutch oven. Add the tenderloins and brown
on all sides. Season with salt and pepper. Add the jam and 2 tablespoons butter
to the Dutch oven. Baste the tenderloins with the butter and jam. Bake at 350
degrees for 30 minutes. Pour the brown sauce over the tenderloins. Bake for
10 minutes or until cooked through, basting occasionally. Garnish with parsley.
   Yield: 8 to 10 servings

Golden Pork Roast

1 (4-pound) pork loin roast
1 tablespoon honey
1 tablespoon soy sauce
1 teaspoon vinegar

1 teaspoon ginger
1 teaspoon dry mustard
1/2 teaspoon salt
1 garlic clove, minced

   Place the roast, fat side up, on a rack in a foil-lined roasting pan. Mix the
honey, soy sauce, vinegar, ginger, dry mustard, salt and garlic in a small bowl.
Brush on all sides of the pork. Roast at 325 degrees for 1 1/2 hours or until a
meat thermometer registers 170 degrees. Brush occasionally with the honey
mixture while roasting.
   Yield: 8 servings

Cranberry-Glazed Pork Roast

2 teaspoons cornstarch
1/4 teaspoon cinnamon
1/8 teaspoon salt
1/2 teaspoon grated orange zest
2 tablespoons orange juice

2 tablespoons dry sherry
1 (16-ounce) can whole cranberry
  sauce
1 (4-pound) boneless pork loin
  roast

Mix the cornstarch, cinnamon, salt, orange zest, orange juice, sherry and cranberry sauce in a small saucepan. Cook, stirring constantly, over medium heat until thickened. Remove from the heat and set aside. Place the pork in a shallow baking dish. Roast at 325 degrees for 45 minutes. Spoon 1/2 cup of the cranberry glaze over the pork. Roast for 30 to 45 minutes or until a meat thermometer registers 145 degrees. Remove from the oven and cover lightly with foil. Let stand for 20 to 30 minutes or until a meat thermometer registers 155 degrees. Serve with the remaining glaze.

Yield: 16 servings

Carolina Slow-Cooker Barbecue

1/2 cup vinegar
1 cup ketchup or barbecue sauce
1/2 cup packed brown sugar

Minced garlic to taste
2 to 3 pounds pork

Mix the vinegar, ketchup, brown sugar and garlic in a slow cooker. Add the pork and turn to coat. Cook on High for 30 minutes. Cook on Low for 8 to 10 hours longer.

Yield: 8 servings

Pork Chops with Almond Plum Sauce

1 cup water
6 tablespoons fresh lemon juice
6 tablespoons soy sauce
1 1/2 teaspoons cornstarch
1/4 teaspoon salt

Pepper to taste
4 (1-inch-thick) pork chops
1 tablespoon vegetable oil
2/3 cup plum jam
1/4 cup sliced almonds, toasted

Mix the water, lemon juice, soy sauce, cornstarch and salt in a bowl. Season with pepper. Place the pork chops in a sealable plastic bag. Add the marinade and seal the bag. Chill for 1 hour. Remove the chops and reserve the marinade. Heat the oil in a skillet. Add the chops and fry for about 3 minutes per side or until browned. Stir in the reserved marinade and plum jam. Simmer for 20 minutes or until cooked through. Sprinkle with almonds before serving.

Yield: 4 servings

Grilled Pork Chops with Barbecue Sauce

1/3 cup Maurice Bessenger's
   barbecue sauce
1/4 cup red wine vinegar
3 tablespoons freshly ground
   horseradish
1/2 teaspoon pepper

1/4 teaspoon garlic powder
Salt to taste
4 to 6 (3/4- to 1-inch-thick)
   boneless pork chops
Olive oil
Pepper to taste

Stir the barbecue sauce, wine vinegar, horseradish, 1/2 teaspoon pepper and garlic powder in a bowl. Season with salt. Coat each side of the pork chops lightly with olive oil and sprinkle with pepper. Place the chops on a preheated grill at medium-high to high heat. Grill for 8 top 10 minutes. Turn and generously coat with the sauce. Grill for 8 to 10 minutes or until cooked through. Coat with more sauce and serve.

Yield: 4 to 6 servings

Sweet-and-Sour Spareribs

1/2 cup finely chopped onion
1/4 cup finely chopped green bell
   pepper
2 (8-ounce) cans tomato sauce
1 (8-ounce) can pineapple tidbits
1/3 cup cider vinegar
1/4 cup packed brown sugar

1 tablespoon
   Worcestershire sauce
1/2 teaspoon dry mustard
Salt and pepper to taste
3 pounds country-style
   pork spareribs

Stir the onion, bell pepper, tomato sauce, pineapple tidbits, vinegar, brown sugar, Worcestershire sauce and dry mustard in a bowl. Season with salt and pepper. Let stand to blend flavors. Arrange the spareribs in a shallow baking pan. Season with salt and pepper. Bake at 350 degrees for 1 1/4 hours. Drain off fat. Pour the sauce evenly over the ribs. Bake for 45 to 50 minutes or until cooked through. Baste frequently during cooking.

Yield: 6 servings

The importance of World War I in Greenville was reflected by a sign that the Chamber of Commerce erected atop a Main Street bank: "Our Country First—Then Greenville."

Marinade for Pork Tenderloin

1 cup honey
1 cup red wine
1 cup soy sauce

1 onion, finely chopped
Minced garlic to taste

Stir the honey, red wine, soy sauce, onion and garlic in a bowl. Place a pork tenderloin(s) in a sealable plastic bag. Add the marinade and seal the bag. Chill for 24 hours, turning the bag occasionally during marinating.

Bombay Chicken

8 boneless skinless chicken breasts
Salt and paprika to taste
1/4 cup flour
1 tablespoon vegetable oil
1 cup sherry

1/4 cup packed brown sugar
2 tablespoons soy sauce
2 tablespoons vegetable oil
1 teaspoon ginger
4 teaspoons sesame seeds

Rinse the chicken breasts and pat dry. Season with salt and paprika and sprinkle with the flour. Heat 1 tablespoon oil in a Dutch oven. Add the chicken and brown on both sides. Mix the sherry, brown sugar, soy sauce, 2 tablespoons oil, ginger and sesame seeds in a bowl. Pour over the chicken. Bake at 375 degrees for 45 minutes or until the chicken is tender and cooked through.
    Yield: 8 servings

Curried Baked Chicken

2 (3- to 3 1/2-pound) chickens,
    cut up
Salt and pepper to taste
1 cup (2 sticks) butter, melted

2 tablespoons curry powder
1 teaspoon paprika
Pinch of ginger

Place the chicken pieces in a shallow roasting pan. Season with salt and pepper. Mix the melted butter, curry powder, paprika and ginger in a bowl. Season with salt and pepper. Pour over the chicken and turn the pieces to coat. Arrange the chicken skin side down. Bake at 350 degrees for 20 minutes, basting often. Turn the chicken and bake for 20 minutes or until cooked through, basting often.
    Yield: 8 servings

Jamaican Chicken

2 pounds boneless chicken breasts,
   cubed
1 (30-ounce) can black beans
1 (8-ounce) can peaches, drained,
   chopped
1/2 cup thinly sliced green onions

1 garlic clove, minced
1 teaspoon ginger
1 teaspoon grated lime zest
2 tablespoons fresh lime juice
1/2 teaspoon salt
Hot cooked rice

    Combine the chicken, beans, peaches, green onions, garlic, ginger, lime zest, lime juice and salt in a large saucepan or electric skillet. Stir to mix. Cover and cook for 1 hour or until the chicken is cooked through. Serve over rice.
    Note: This recipe may be made in a slow cooker.
    Yield: 4 servings

Katie's Lemon Chicken (Katie Couric)

4 boneless skinless chicken breasts
Flour
2 tablespoons butter
2 tablespoons olive oil
3 tablespoons flour
Juice of 2 lemons

3 cups chicken broth
Salt and white pepper to taste
Hot cooked basmati rice
Fresh chopped parsley and lemon
   slices for garnish

    Pound the chicken breasts on a work surface to a uniform thickness. Dredge lightly in flour and shake off any excess. Heat the butter and olive oil in a large skillet over medium-high heat until sizzling. Add the chicken and sauté until cooked through. Remove the chicken to a plate. Whisk 3 tablespoons flour in the skillet for 1 minute or until boiling. Whisk in the lemon juice and chicken broth. Reduce the heat to simmer. Return the chicken to the skillet. Cook until the sauce thickens and the chicken is heated through. Season with salt and white pepper. Serve the chicken on a bed of basmati rice and spoon the sauce over the chicken. Garnish with parsley and lemon slices.
    Yield: 4 servings

Italian Baked Chicken

1/2 cup seasoned bread crumbs
2 whole chicken breasts, skinned,
   boned, halved, flattened
2 tablespoons olive oil

2 tomatoes, sliced 1/2-inch thick
Fresh basil leaves, sliced in ribbons
4 slices provolone cheese
2 tablespoons chopped fresh parsley

Spread the bread crumbs in a flat dish. Add the chicken and press the crumbs onto both sides. Heat the olive oil in a skillet over medium-high heat. Add the chicken and brown on both sides. Remove to a lightly oiled baking dish and arrange in a single layer. Let cool. Top the chicken with the sliced tomatoes. Sprinkle with basil leaves and top with the cheese slices. Sprinkle with the parsley. Bake at 400 degrees for 20 minutes or until the chicken is cooked through.

Yield: 4 servings

Classic Chicken Divan

2 bunches fresh broccoli, or
   2 (10-ounce) packages frozen
   broccoli spears
1/4 cup (1/2 stick) butter
1/4 cup flour
2 cups chicken broth
1/2 cup heavy cream

3 tablespoons cooking sherry
1/2 teaspoon salt
Dash of pepper
3 chicken breasts, cooked, sliced
1/4 cup grated Parmesan cheese
Additional Parmesan cheese
Spiced peaches for garnish

Cook the broccoli in boiling salted water; drain well. Arrange the spears crosswise in a 9×13-inch baking dish. Melt the butter in a saucepan. Stir in the flour. Add the chicken broth all at once and cook, stirring constantly, until thickened. Stir in the cream, sherry, salt and pepper. Pour half the sauce over the broccoli. Top with the sliced chicken. Stir the 1/4 cup Parmesan cheese into the remaining sauce. Pour over the chicken and sprinkle with additional Parmesan cheese. Bake at 350 degrees for 30 minutes or until hot. Place under the broiler until the sauce is golden brown. Garnish with spiced peaches.

Yield: 6 to 8 servings

Oven-Fried Chicken

3 pounds chicken pieces
1/4 cup shortening
1/4 cup (1/2 stick) butter
1/2 cup flour

1 teaspoon salt
1 teaspoon paprika
1/4 teaspoon pepper

Rinse the chicken and pat dry. Melt the shortening and butter in a 9×13-inch baking pan in a 425-degree oven. Mix the flour, salt, paprika and pepper in a shallow dish. Coat the chicken with the flour mixture. Arrange the chicken skin side down in the baking pan. Bake at 425 degrees for 30 minutes. Turn the chicken and bake for 30 minutes or until cooked through.
Yield: 6 servings

Stir-Fry Chicken

3 tablespoons soy sauce
1 tablespoon cornstarch
2 tablespoons olive oil
1 garlic clove, minced
2 teaspoons grated fresh gingerroot
1 pound chicken breasts, cut into
    bite-size pieces

2 tablespoons olive oil
2 small onions, cut into 6 wedges
1 red bell pepper, cut into strips
3 cups broccoli florets
2 carrots, sliced diagonally
1/2 cup chicken broth
Hot cooked rice

Mix the soy sauce and cornstarch in a small bowl until smooth. Heat 2 tablespoons olive oil in a wok or large deep skillet over high heat until very hot. Add the garlic and gingerroot and stir-fry for 1 minute. Add the chicken and stir-fry for 3 minutes or until browned. Remove the chicken with a slotted spoon to a bowl. Add 2 tablespoons olive oil to the wok and heat until very hot. Add the onions and bell pepper and stir-fry for 2 minutes. Add the broccoli and carrots and stir-fry for 2 minutes or until tender-crisp. Add the cooked chicken. Add the broth slowly to the wok. Stir in the soy sauce mixture. Bring to a boil, stirring constantly. Cook until the sauce thickens. Serve over rice.
Yield: 4 servings

Chicken Pot Pie

6 tablespoons margarine
4 cups chopped cooked chicken
   (about 4 chicken breasts)
1 (10 3/4-ounce) can cream of
   chicken soup
1 1/4 cups chicken broth

1 (16-ounce) package frozen
   vegetables such as peas, carrots or
   mixed vegetables
1 cup buttermilk baking mix
1 cup milk

Melt the margarine in a 9×13-inch baking pan in a 425-degree oven. Top with the cooked chicken. Mix the cream of chicken soup and chicken broth in a bowl. Pour over the chicken. Top with the frozen vegetables. Stir the baking mix and milk in a bowl until well blended. Pour over the vegetables. Bake at 425 degrees for 25 to 35 minutes.

Yield: 8 servings

Chicken Roll-Ups

2 tablespoons butter
3 tablespoons olive oil
6 mushrooms, chopped
1 onion, chopped
2 garlic cloves, minced
3 dashes of Worcestershire sauce

1/4 cup white wine
1/4 cup seasoned bread crumbs
6 boneless skinless chicken breasts,
   pounded into 1/4-inch thickness
6 slices ham
6 slices Swiss cheese

Heat the butter and olive oil in a skillet. Add the mushrooms, onions, garlic, Worcestershire sauce and wine. Sauté until the vegetables are softened. Remove from the heat. Add the bread crumbs and mix well. Arrange the chicken on a work surface. Top each with a slice of ham, a slice of Swiss cheese and 1/6 of the mushroom mixture. Roll up and fasten with 3 wooden picks or string. Grill on foil on a preheated grill for 8 to 10 minutes or until the chicken is cooked through. Turn during grilling to prevent sticking.

Yield: 6 servings

Cornish Hens in White Wine

4 Cornish game hens, cut in half
4 ounces bacon
15 small white onions
2 tablespoons butter
1/4 cup cognac or brandy
4 shallots, coarsely chopped
4 ounces sliced mushrooms
1/4 garlic clove, minced

Bouquet garni
1 1/2 teaspoons salt
1/2 teaspoon pepper
1 teaspoon sugar
1/4 teaspoon nutmeg
2 cups dry red wine
1 cup dry white wine
Fresh chopped parsley

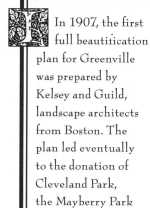

In 1907, the first full beautiiication plan for Greenville was prepared by Kelsey and Guild, landscape architects from Boston. The plan led eventually to the donation of Cleveland Park, the Mayberry Park baseball field, Reedy Falls historic park, and the Broad Street Connector.

Rinse the hens and pat dry. Fry the bacon in a 6-quart saucepan over medium heat until crisp. Remove with a slotted spoon to paper towels to drain. Crumble when cool. Add the onions to the bacon drippings. Cook for 5 minutes, stirring occasionally. Remove with a slotted spoon to a bowl. Add the butter to the saucepan and heat over medium heat until hot. Add the hens and brown on all sides. Heat the cognac in a small pan. Ignite the cognac when vapors rise. Pour the flaming cognac over the hens. Remove the hens to a platter.

Add the shallots, mushrooms, garlic, bouquet garni, salt, pepper, sugar and nutmeg to the saucepan. Stir to mix. Cover and simmer over very low heat for 5 minutes. Stir in the red and white wine. Return the hens to the saucepan. Bring to a boil, reduce the heat and cover. Simmer for 30 minutes. Add the onions and simmer for 25 minutes or until the onions are tender and the hens are cooked through. Remove the bouquet garni. Serve the hens garnished with the crumbled bacon and chopped parsley.

Note: Combine parsley, thyme and a bay leaf tied in cheesecloth or in a tea holder to make a bouquet garni.

Yield: 8 servings

Jambalaya

2 onions, chopped
2 ribs celery, chopped
2 bell peppers, chopped
2 garlic cloves, chopped
2 tablespoons vegetable oil
1/2 cup flour
2 (28-ounce) cans whole tomatoes
1 teaspoon thyme
2 bay leaves
2 boneless chicken breasts,
    cut into pieces

1 pound smoked sausage,
    cut into pieces
1 tablespoon hot red pepper sauce
1 tablespoon Worcestershire sauce
1/2 teaspoon cayenne pepper
8 ounces shrimp, peeled, deveined
Hot cooked rice
2 sweet potatoes, cooked, sliced, for
    garnish
Chopped fresh parsley for garnish

Sauté the onions, celery, bell peppers and garlic in a large nonstick saucepan until softened. Add the oil and flour. Cook, stirring constantly, until it begins to brown. Stir in the tomatoes, thyme and bay leaves, breaking up the tomatoes with a spoon. Add the chicken, sausage, pepper sauce, Worcestershire sauce and cayenne. Stir to mix.

Cover and simmer for 1 hour. Add the shrimp. Cook until the shrimp turn pink. Remove the bay leaves. Serve over the rice. Top with the slices of cooked sweet potatoes and chopped parsley.

Yield: 8 servings

Baked Flounder with Tomatoes and Garlic

2 tablespoons olive oil
2 (6-ounce) flounder fillets
Salt and pepper to taste

1 large tomato, seeded, chopped
1 tablespoon minced garlic
1 tablespoon chopped fresh parsley

Brush a small amount of the olive oil in a small shallow baking dish. Arrange the fillets in the baking dish and season with salt and pepper. Mix the remaining olive oil, tomato and garlic in a bowl. Spoon over the fillets. Bake at 400 degrees for 15 minutes or until the fish flakes easily. Sprinkle with the parsley and serve.
Yield: 2 servings

Pecan-Coated Baked Salmon

4 (4- to 6-ounce) salmon fillets
1/8 teaspoon salt
1/8 teaspoon pepper
2 tablespoons Dijon mustard
2 tablespoons butter, melted
1 1/2 tablespoons honey

1/4 cup soft bread crumbs
1/4 cup finely chopped pecans
2 teaspoons chopped fresh parsley
Fresh parsley sprigs and lemon
  slices for garnish

Arrange the salmon fillets in a shallow baking dish. Sprinkle with the salt and pepper. Mix the mustard, melted butter and honey in a small bowl. Brush on the fillets. Mix the bread crumbs, pecans and parsley in a small bowl. Spoon evenly on top of the fillets. Bake at 450 degrees for 10 minutes or until the fish flakes easily. Garnish with parsley sprigs and lemon slices.
Yield: 4 servings

Pesto-Crusted Salmon

Pesto
2 garlic cloves, minced
2 tablespoons pine nuts
6 cups lightly packed fresh basil
    leaves
1/2 cup olive oil
1 cup fresh bread crumbs
Salt and freshly ground pepper
    to taste

Salmon
6 (6-ounce) skinless salmon fillets
Salt and freshly ground pepper
    to taste
2 teaspoons olive oil
1/2 cup fresh bread crumbs
2 teaspoons olive oil
1 tablespoon unsalted butter, cut
    into 6 pieces

For the pesto, combine the garlic and pine nuts in a food processor container and pulse to a paste. Add the basil leaves and process to a paste. Add 1/2 cup olive oil slowly with the machine running to make a smooth paste. Stop the machine once during processing to scrape down the sides. Remove to a bowl. Stir in 1 cup bread crumbs. Season with salt and pepper.

For the salmon, sprinkle the salmon fillets with salt and pepper. Heat the 2 teaspoons of olive oil in a large skillet over high heat until almost smoking. Add 3 fillets to the skillet and cook for 1 minute per side or until browned. Remove to a plate. Repeat with the remaining 3 fillets. Let the salmon cool to room temperature.

Spread 2 tablespoons of pesto on one side of each fillet. Divide 1/2 cup bread crumbs between the fillets and gently pat onto the pesto. Divide 2 teaspoons olive oil between 2 ovenproof skillets. Heat the oil over medium heat until hot. Add 3 fillets per skillet, pesto side down. Add 1 piece of butter next to each fillet. Cook for 3 minutes or until the bread crumbs are toasted. Place the skillets in a 350-degree oven. Bake for 5 minutes or until the fish flakes easily. Serve with the pesto side up.

Yield: 6 servings

Crab Cakes with Avocado Tartare Sauce

Avocado Tartare Sauce
1 cup mayonnaise
2 ripe avocados, peeled, pitted, chopped
2 tablespoons capers, chopped
4 gherkin pickles, chopped
1 tablespoon chopped fresh parsley
1 tablespoon chopped fresh chives
1 teaspoon chopped fresh thyme
Cayenne pepper to taste
Lemon juice to taste
Coarse sea salt to taste
Freshly ground black pepper
   to taste

Crab Cakes
1/4 cup mayonnaise
1 egg, beaten
4 green onions, thinly sliced
1 tablespoon chopped fresh parsley
1 tablespoon chopped fresh chives
6 tablespoons lemon juice
1/4 teaspoon Worcestershire sauce
1 tablespoon Old Bay seasoning
1 teaspoon cayenne pepper
Coarse sea salt to taste
Freshly ground black pepper
   to taste
1 pound jumbo lump crab meat
1 1/2 cups bread crumbs
1/4 cup peanut or vegetable oil

For the sauce, mix the mayonnaise, avocados, capers, pickles, parsley, chives and thyme in a bowl. Season with cayenne pepper, lemon juice, salt and black pepper. Remove to a serving bowl and cover. Chill until ready to serve.

For the crab cakes, mix the mayonnaise, egg, green onions, parsley, chives, lemon juice, Worcestershire sauce, Old Bay seasoning, cayenne, salt and black pepper. Fold in the crab meat gently, leaving the lumps intact. Shape the mixture into 8 cakes. Spread the bread crumbs in a shallow dish. Coat each cake with the crumbs. Arrange on a plate and chill for 30 minutes. Heat the oil in a large skillet. Add the crab cakes and cook for 2 to 3 minutes per side or until golden brown. Remove to paper towels to drain. Serve with the Avocado Tartare Sauce.

Yield: 4 servings

Carolina Barbecue Shrimp with Creamy White Cheddar Grits

Grits
5 cups chicken stock
1 to 2 teaspoons salt
1 to 2 teaspoons pepper
1 cup stone ground white grits
1/2 cup finely chopped green
  bell pepper
1/2 cup finely chopped red
  bell pepper
1/2 cup finely chopped yellow
  bell pepper
1/2 cup finely chopped red onion
1/2 cup heavy cream (optional)
1/2 cup shredded white Cheddar
  cheese

Barbecued Shrimp
2 tablespoons extra-virgin olive oil
28 medium shrimp, peeled,
  deveined
1/2 cup chopped red bell pepper
1/2 cup sliced green onions
2 fresh rosemary sprigs
1 tablespoon chopped garlic
1 lemon, sliced, seeded
Salt and pepper to taste
1/4 cup shrimp stock
1/2 cup white wine
1/4 cup Worcestershire sauce
1/2 cup (1 stick) unsalted butter,
  softened

For the grits, heat the chicken stock to boiling in a medium saucepan. Stir in the salt and pepper. Whisk in the grits. Reduce the heat to medium-low. Simmer for about 15 minutes, whisking occasionally. Stir in the bell peppers and onion. Whisk in the cream. Simmer for 5 minutes. Add the cheese and stir until melted. Keep warm until serving time.

For the shrimp, heat the olive oil in a large skillet over medium-high heat. Add the shrimp, bell pepper, onions, rosemary and garlic. Add the lemon slices, squeezing as added. Season with salt and pepper. Sauté for 1 minute. Stir in the stock and wine. Cook until reduced by half. Add the Worcestershire sauce and remove from the heat. Whisk in the butter until melted. Season with salt and pepper. Serve over the hot Creamy White Cheddar Grits.

Yield: 4 servings

Shrimp Creole with Cheese Rice

1/2 cup olive oil
1/2 cup chopped uncooked bacon
2 garlic cloves, chopped
2/3 cup chopped celery
1 bell pepper, chopped
1 large onion, chopped
2 (16-ounce) cans diced tomatoes
2 (6-ounce) cans tomato paste
1 cup water
2 teaspoons Worcestershire sauce

1/2 teaspoon Tabasco sauce
4 cups water
2 cups white rice
1 onion, finely chopped
1 cup sharp Cheddar cheese
2 1/2 pounds shrimp, peeled, deveined

Heat the olive oil in a large skillet. Add the bacon, garlic, celery, bell pepper and large onion. Sauté until the vegetables are softened. Stir in the tomatoes, tomato paste, 1 cup water, Worcestershire sauce and Tabasco sauce. Reduce the heat and simmer for 3 hours.

Heat 4 cups of water in a medium saucepan to boiling. Stir in the rice and finely chopped onion. Reduce the heat and cover. Simmer for 20 minutes or until the liquid is absorbed and the rice is tender. Add the cheese and stir until melted. Add the shrimp to the tomato mixture. Cook for 10 minutes or until the shrimp turn pink. Arrange the rice on a large serving platter in a ring shape. Spoon the Shrimp Creole into the center and serve.

Note: The tomato mixture can be frozen before adding the shrimp.

Yield: 8 servings

In 1915, the first Southern Textile Exposition was staged in the warehouses of the Piedmont and Northern Railway on West Washington Street. This 1915 show began a long and successful tradition in Greenville. Greenville declared itself the "Textile Center of the South." Today, the Greenville's Palmetto Exposition Center hosts the American Textile Machinery Exhibition International.

Shrimp and Wild Rice Casserole

1/4 cup (1/2 stick) butter
1/2 cup thinly sliced onion
1/2 to 1 cup sliced mushrooms
1 tablespoon Worcestershire sauce
Few drops of Tabasco sauce
1 package long grain & wild rice,
    prepared according to package
    directions

1 pound peeled cooked shrimp
1 tablespoon butter
1 tablespoon flour
1 cup hot chicken broth
Salt and pepper to taste

    Melt the 1/4 cup butter in a skillet. Add the onion and mushrooms and sauté until softened. Remove from the heat and stir in the Worcestershire sauce, Tabasco sauce, cooked rice and shrimp. Melt the 1 tablespoon butter in a saucepan. Add the flour and stir until smooth. Whisk in the chicken broth. Cook, whisking constantly, until slightly thickened. Season with salt and pepper. Stir into the rice mixture. Spoon into a buttered baking dish.

    Bake at 300 degrees for 30 minutes or until heated through.

    Note: This recipe can be made 1 day before baking. Cover and chill. Increase baking time if removed directly from refrigerator to the oven.

    Yield: 6 servings

Shrimp in Feta Cheese

1 1/2 tablespoons butter
1 1/2 tablespoons vegetable oil
1/2 cup finely chopped onion
1/2 cup dry white wine
4 medium tomatoes, peeled, chopped
1 small garlic clove, minced
1 teaspoon salt

1/4 teaspoon pepper
3/4 teaspoon oregano
4 ounces feta cheese, crumbled
1 pound large shrimp, peeled, deveined
1/4 cup chopped fresh parsley

 Greenville's sister city is Bergamo, capital of Bergamo Provincia in the Lombardy region of northern Italy.

Heat the butter and vegetable oil in a heavy skillet. Add the onion and sauté until softened. Stir in the wine, tomatoes, garlic, salt, pepper and oregano. Bring to a boil. Reduce the heat to medium and simmer until the sauce is slightly thickened.

Stir in the feta cheese and simmer for 10 to 15 minutes. Add additional seasonings, if desired. Stir in the shrimp and cook for 5 minutes or until the shrimp turn pink, do not overcook. Garnish with the parsley and serve in large bowls with crusty French bread.

Yield: 4 servings

Cakes & Pies

Buttermilk Blackberry Jam Cake

Cake
2 eggs plus 1 egg yolk
1 cup packed brown sugar
1 cup buttermilk
1 cup blackberry jam (or other
    favorite flavor)
2 1/2 cups cake flour
2 teaspoons baking powder
1 teaspoon baking soda
1/2 teaspoon cinnamon
1/4 teaspoon nutmeg
Pinch of salt
3/4 cup (1 1/2 sticks) butter, melted

Seven-Minute Frosting
1 egg white
1 cup sugar
3/4 cup water
1/4 teaspoon cream of tartar
1 teaspoon vanilla extract

For the cake, beat the eggs and egg yolk in a mixing bowl until light. Beat in the brown sugar, buttermilk and jam. Sift the flour, baking powder and baking soda into a bowl. Stir in cinnamon, nutmeg and salt. Beat the dry ingredients gradually into the egg mixture. Add the melted butter and beat well. Pour into 2 greased and floured 9-inch round cake pans. Bake at 375 degrees for 30 minutes or until a wooden pick inserted in the center comes out clean. Cool in the pans for 10 minutes. Remove to a wire rack to cool completely. Frost with Seven-Minute Frosting when cool.

For the frosting, combine the egg white, sugar, water and cream of tartar in the top of a double boiler over boiling water. Beat with a hand-held mixer for 7 minutes. Replace the boiling water in the bottom of the double boiler with cold water. Let the frosting stand over the cold water for 5 minutes. Stir in the vanilla.

Yield: 8 servings

Fresh Apple Cake

3 eggs
2 cups sugar
1 1/2 cups vegetable oil
1/3 cup orange juice
3 cups flour
1 teaspoon baking soda
1 teaspoon cinnamon
1/4 teaspoon salt
1 teaspoon vanilla extract

2 cups chopped peeled
   cooking apples
1 cup flaked coconut
1 cup chopped nuts
1/2 cup (1 stick) margarine
1/2 teaspoon baking soda
1 cup sugar
1/2 cup buttermilk

Beat the eggs, 2 cups sugar, oil and orange juice in a large bowl. Sift the flour, 1 teaspoon baking soda, cinnamon and salt into a separate bowl. Add to the egg mixture and stir to mix well. Stir in the vanilla, apples, coconut and nuts. Pour into a greased and floured 10-inch tube pan.

Bake at 350 degrees for 1 hour or until a wooden pick inserted in the center comes out clean. Remove to a wire rack.

Melt the margarine in a saucepan. Stir in 1/2 teaspoon baking soda, 1 cup sugar and the buttermilk. Bring to a rolling boil, stirring frequently. Pour over the hot cake. Let cool in the pan for 1 hour before removing to a serving plate.

Yield: 12 servings

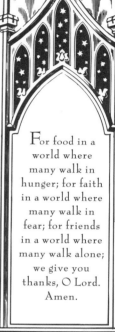

For food in a world where many walk in hunger; for faith in a world where many walk in fear; for friends in a world where many walk alone; we give you thanks, O Lord. Amen.

Caramel Cake

Cake
2 3/4 cups flour
2 teaspoons baking powder
1/2 teaspoon salt
1 cup sour cream
1/4 cup milk
1 cup (2 sticks) butter, softened
2 cups sugar
4 eggs
1 teaspoon vanilla extract
1 teaspoon rum extract (optional)

Caramel Frosting
2 1/2 cups sugar
3/4 cup milk
1 egg, slightly beaten
Pinch of salt
1/2 cup (1 stick) butter,
  cut into pieces
1/2 cup sugar

For the cake, mix the flour, baking powder and salt in a bowl. Mix the sour cream and milk in a small bowl. Beat the butter in a mixing bowl at medium speed until fluffy. Beat in the sugar gradually. Beat in the eggs 1 at a time. Add in the dry ingredients alternately with the sour cream mixture, beating well after each addition. Stir in the vanilla and rum extract. Pour into 2 greased and floured 9-inch round cake pans. Bake at 350 degrees for 30 to 35 minutes or until a wooden pick inserted in the center comes out clean. Cool in the pans for 10 minutes. Remove to a wire rack to cool completely. Frost with Caramel Frosting when cool.

For the frosting, mix 2 1/2 cups sugar, the milk, egg and salt in a bowl. Stir in the butter. Sprinkle 1/2 cup sugar in a heavy saucepan. Cook, stirring constantly, over medium heat until the sugar melts and the syrup is a light golden brown. Remove from the heat and stir in the butter mixture. Return the lumpy mixture to medium heat. Cook, stirring often, until a candy thermometer registers 235 degrees, about 15 to 20 minutes. Remove from the heat and let cool for 5 minutes. Beat with a wooden spoon for 5 minutes or until of a spreading consistency.

Yield: 8 servings

Carrot Cake with Cream Cheese Frosting

Cake
2 cups sugar
1 1/2 cups vegetable oil
4 eggs
2 cups flour
2 teaspoons baking soda
2 teaspoons cinnamon
1/2 teaspoon salt
3 cups grated carrots
1/2 cup chopped walnuts or
    pecans

Cream Cheese Frosting
8 ounces cream cheese,
    softened
1/4 cup (1/2 stick)
    butter, softened
2 teaspoons pure vanilla
    extract
1 (1-pound) package
    confectioners' sugar,
    sifted if lumpy
Milk (optional)

 "Miss Jim" Perry, a Greenville native and 1917 graduate of the University of California Law School, returned to make Greenville her permanent home. In 1918, she became the first woman admitted to the practice of law in South Carolina.

For the cake, beat the sugar and oil in a mixing bowl until well blended. Add the eggs and beat until creamy. Sift the flour, baking soda, cinnamon and salt into a bowl. Add to the egg mixture and beat well. Fold in the carrots and walnuts. Spread in a greased and floured 9×13-inch baking pan. Bake at 350 degrees for 40 to 45 minutes or until a wooden pick inserted in the center comes out clean. Remove to a wire rack. Frost with Cream Cheese Frosting when cool.

For the frosting, beat the cream cheese and butter in a mixing bowl until fluffy. Beat in the vanilla. Beat in the confectioners' sugar gradually. Add more confectioners' sugar for a thicker frosting or add a little milk for a thinner frosting.

Yield: 12 servings

Chocolate Fontaine (The Palms)

5 eggs
2/3 cup sugar
1 cup flour
1/3 cup baking cocoa
2 tablespoons butter, melted, cooled
1 1/4 cups heavy cream
1 teaspoon cinnamon
10 1/2 ounces bittersweet chocolate

1 cup sugar
1 cup water
1/4 cup raspberry-flavored liqueur
1 pint raspberries
15 sheets phyllo dough
Melted butter
Sugar
1 pint vanilla ice cream

Combine the eggs and 2/3 cup sugar in the top of a double boiler over simmering water. Beat with a hand-held electric mixer until light and fluffy. Remove to a bowl and let cool to lukewarm. Mix the flour and baking cocoa in a small bowl. Fold into the egg mixture. Fold in the melted butter. Pour into a greased and floured 10-inch round cake pan. Bake at 350 degrees for 20 minutes or until the cake springs back when touched. Cool in the pan for 10 minutes. Remove to a wire rack to cool completely.

Heat the cream in a heavy saucepan until boiling. Whisk in the cinnamon. Remove from the heat and add the chocolate. Stir until smooth. Let cool until thick. Heat 1 cup sugar and the water in a heavy saucepan until boiling. Remove from the heat and stir in the raspberry liqueur. Let cool. Cut the cake into 7 little cakes with a 3-inch round cutter. Brush both sides of each cake with the raspberry syrup. Spread the top with a thin layer of the chocolate ganache. Arrange the raspberries on top; set on a plate. Chill for 30 minutes or until set.

Place 1 sheet of phyllo on a work surface. Brush with melted butter and sprinkle with sugar. Top with another sheet of phyllo and brush with melted butter and sprinkle with sugar. Cut into 4 equal rectangles and stack together. Place one chilled cake in the center of the phyllo stack. Fold the dough over the cake and brush with melted butter. Repeat with the remaining 6 cakes and 12 sheets of phyllo dough. Arrange on a baking sheet. Cut the remaining sheet of phyllo dough into strips and arrange on the baking sheet. Bake at 350 degrees for 7 minutes or until golden brown. Remove to 7 dessert plates. Garnish with raspberries, baked phyllo strips and a scoop of vanilla ice cream. Serve warm.

Yield: 7 servings

Decadent Double-Chocolate Brownie Torte

5 ounces unsweetened chocolate
1/2 cup (1 stick) unsalted butter
1 1/2 cups sugar
4 eggs
1 teaspoon pure vanilla extract
1/4 cup flour
2 ounces bittersweet chocolate, chopped

3 ounces white chocolate, chopped
1/4 cup finely ground toasted pecans
1 cup whipping cream, whipped or 1 quart vanilla ice cream
Fresh seasonal berries

Combine the unsweetened chocolate and butter in a metal bowl. Place over a saucepan of simmering water until the chocolate is melted. Remove from the heat. Beat the sugar and eggs in a mixing bowl at high speed for 5 minutes or until thick and pale yellow. Reduce the speed to medium and beat in the melted chocolate. Scrape down the sides of the bowl. Beat in the vanilla. Add the flour gradually and beat until just blended. Remove the bowl let stand for 5 minutes. Fold in the bittersweet chocolate, white chocolate and pecans. Pour into a 9-inch cake pan lined with parchment paper in the bottom.

Bake at 350 degrees for 30 to 35 minutes or until a wooden pick inserted in the center comes out clean. Cool in the pan for 10 minutes. Run a knife around the edge of the pan. Invert onto a platter. Cut into individual portions and arrange on dessert plates. Serve warm with whipped cream or ice cream and top with berries.

Yield: 10 servings

Bête Noire

1/2 cup water

1 cup sugar

8 ounces unsweetened chocolate, finely chopped

4 ounces semisweet chocolate, finely chopped

1 cup (2 sticks) butter, softened, cut into small pieces

5 extra-large eggs

1/3 cup sugar

Combine the water and 1 cup sugar in a heavy 2-quart saucepan. Bring to a boil over high heat. Cook, stirring often, until a candy thermometer registers 220 degrees, about 4 minutes. Remove from the heat and add the unsweetened chocolate and semisweet chocolate. Stir until the chocolate is melted. Add the butter gradually, stirring until the butter is melted and the mixture is smooth.

Beat the eggs and 1/3 cup sugar in a mixing bowl at high speed for 15 minutes or until pale yellow and tripled in volume. Reduce the speed to low and beat in the chocolate mixture just until blended. Pour into a 9-inch cake pan lined with a circle of parchment paper in the bottom. Set into a slightly larger pan. Pour boiling water into the larger pan.

Bake at 350 degrees for 25 minutes or until a wooden pick inserted in the center comes out clean. Do not bake for more than 35 minutes. Cool in the pan for 10 minutes. Run a knife around the edge of the pan. Invert onto a baking sheet. Place a serving plate on top of the cake and invert again so that the cake is right side up on the serving plate. Serve warm or at room temperature.

Yield: 6 to 8 servings

The Best Coconut Cake

1 (2-layer) package butter-flavored
    cake mix
3 eggs
2/3 cup water
1/2 cup (1 stick) butter, softened
1 (9-ounce) package frozen flaked
    coconut
2 teaspoons coconut flavoring
1 (14-ounce) can sweetened
    condensed milk

1 1/2 cups confectioners'
    sugar
2 teaspoons vanilla
    extract
2 teaspoons coconut
    flavoring
Whipped topping

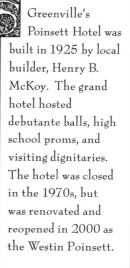

Greenville's Poinsett Hotel was built in 1925 by local builder, Henry B. McKoy. The grand hotel hosted debutante balls, high school proms, and visiting dignitaries. The hotel was closed in the 1970s, but was renovated and reopened in 2000 as the Westin Poinsett.

    Beat the cake mix, eggs, water and butter in a mixing bowl at medium speed according to the cake mix directions. Remove a small amount of coconut from the package and set aside for garnishing. Add the remaining coconut and 2 teaspoons coconut flavoring to the batter. Beat until mixed. Pour into a 9×13-inch greased and floured baking pan.

    Bake according to the cake mix directions. Remove to a wire rack. Poke holes in the surface of the cake with a fork. Beat the sweetened condensed milk, confectioners' sugar, vanilla and 2 teaspoons coconut flavoring in a mixing bowl. Add enough water to equal 2 cups. Pour over the hot cake and spread evenly. Let cool. Top with whipped topping and garnish with the reserved coconut. Store in the refrigerator.

    Yield: 12 servings

Old-Fashioned Soft Gingerbread with Spiced Lemon Sauce

Gingerbread
1/2 cup (1 stick) butter, softened
3/4 cup sugar
1 egg
1 cup molasses
2 1/2 cups sifted flour
1 1/2 teaspoons baking soda
1/2 teaspoon salt
1 teaspoon cinnamon
4 teaspoons ginger
1 teaspoon ground cloves
1 cup hot water

Spiced Lemon Sauce
1/2 cup sugar
1 1/2 tablespoons cornstarch
1 teaspoon nutmeg
1 teaspoon cinnamon
Pinch of salt
1 cup boiling water
1 teaspoon grated lemon zest
3 tablespoons lemon juice
1 tablespoon margarine

For the gingerbread, cream the butter and sugar in a large mixing bowl until light and fluffy. Beat in the egg and molasses. Mix the flour, baking soda, salt, cinnamon, ginger and cloves in a bowl. Add to the molasses mixture and beat until smooth. Add the hot water and stir until well mixed. Pour into a greased 9×13-inch baking pan. Bake at 350 degrees for 35 minutes or until a wooden pick inserted in the center comes out clean. Serve warm with the Spiced Lemon Sauce.

For the sauce, mix the sugar, cornstarch, nutmeg, cinnamon and salt in a microwave-safe bowl. Stir in the boiling water. Microwave on High until thick. Add the lemon zest, lemon juice and margarine. Stir until the margarine is melted.

Yield: 12 servings

Orange Cream Cake

1 (2-layer) package yellow cake mix
1 envelope whipped topping mix
3/4 cup fat-free mayonnaise
2 teaspoons grated orange zest

8 ounces cream cheese, softened
1 tablespoons grated orange zest
1 cup confectioners' sugar

Beat the cake mix, whipped topping mix, mayonnaise and 2 teaspoons orange zest in a mixing bowl for 2 minutes. Pour into a bundt pan coated with nonstick cooking spray. Bake at 350 degrees for 35 to 40 minutes or until a wooden pick inserted in the center comes out clean. Cool in the pan for 10 minutes. Invert onto a wire rack to cool completely. Beat the cream cheese and 1 tablespoon orange zest in a medium mixing bowl until fluffy. Beat in the confectioners' sugar gradually. Beat until well mixed. Spread the frosting over the cake.

Yield: 10 servings

Cotton Picking Cake

1 (2-layer) package butter-flavored
  yellow cake mix
1 (3-ounce) package vanilla instant
  pudding mix
4 eggs
1/2 cup vegetable oil
1 1/2 cups chopped pecans

1 (16-ounce) can mandarin
  oranges, drained
1 (20-ounce) can crushed pineapple
1 (6-ounce) package vanilla instant
  pudding mix
8 ounces whipped topping

Beat the cake mix, 3-ounce pudding mix, eggs and oil in a mixing bowl at medium speed according to cake mix directions. Stir in the pecans and mandarin oranges. Pour into 3 greased and floured 8-inch round cake pans. Bake at 350 degrees for 35 minutes or until the layers test done. Cool in the pans for 10 minutes. Invert onto a wire rack to cool completely. Mix the pineapple and 6-ounce pudding mix in a bowl with a fork. Fold in the whipped topping. Spread between the cake layers and on the top of the cake.

Yield: 8 servings

Brown Sugar Pound Cake

1 1/2 cups (3 sticks) margarine,
  softened
1 cup sugar
2 1/4 cups packed brown sugar
5 eggs
3 cups flour

1/2 teaspoon baking powder
1 cup milk
1 teaspoon vanilla extract
1 cup chopped nuts dredged in
  2 tablespoons flour

Beat the margarine, sugar and brown sugar in a mixing bowl at medium speed until light and fluffy. Beat in the eggs 1 at a time. Sift the flour and baking powder into a bowl. Add the dry ingredients to the margarine mixture alternately with the milk, beginning and ending with the dry ingredients. Reduce the speed to low and add the vanilla and nuts. Beat until mixed. Pour into a greased and floured 10-inch tube pan. Bake at 325 degrees for 1 1/2 hours or until a wooden pick inserted in the center comes out clean.

Yield: 10 servings

Cream Cheese Pound Cake

1 cup (2 sticks) butter, softened
8 ounces cream cheese, softened
2 cups sugar
2 cups flour

2 teaspoons baking powder
6 eggs
2 teaspoons vanilla extract
Confectioners' sugar

Cream the butter, cream cheese and sugar in a mixing bowl until light and fluffy. Sift the flour and baking powder into a bowl. Add the dry ingredients alternately with the eggs, beating well after each addition. Stir in the vanilla. Pour into a greased and floured 10-inch tube pan. Bake at 350 degrees for 1 hour or until a wooden pick inserted in the center comes out clean. Remove to a wire rack and let cool in the pan. Remove to a serving plate. Dust with confectioners' sugar.

Yield: 12 servings

Pineapple Pound Cake

2 cups shortening
3 cups sugar
8 eggs
3 cups flour

Dash of salt
1 teaspoon vanilla extract
1 (8-ounce) can crushed pineapple

Cream the shortening and sugar in a mixing bowl until light and fluffy. Add the eggs 1 at a time, beating well after each addition. Beat in the flour and salt gradually. Stir in the vanilla. Drain the pineapple and add the juice to the batter. Beat until well mixed. Fold in the drained pineapple. Pour into a greased and floured 10-inch tube pan. Bake at 350 degrees for 1 hour or until a wooden pick inserted in the center comes out clean. Remove to a wire rack to cool.

Yield: 12 servings

Million-Dollar Pound Cake

2 cups (4 sticks) margarine,
   softened
3 cups sugar
6 eggs, at room temperature
4 cups flour
3/4 cup milk
1 teaspoon vanilla extract

1 teaspoon almond extract
1 teaspoon lemon extract
6 tablespoons margarine, softened
1 (1-pound) package confectioners'
   sugar
1/4 cup milk or lemon juice

Cream 2 cups margarine and the sugar in a bowl until light and fluffy. Add the eggs 1 at a time, beating well after each addition. Add the flour alternately with 3/4 cup milk, beating well after each addition. Stir in the vanilla, almond extract and lemon extract. Pour into a greased and floured 10-inch tube pan. Bake at 350 degrees for 1 hour and 40 minutes or until a wooden pick inserted in the center comes out clean. Remove to a wire rack and let cool in the pan. Remove to a serving plate. Beat 6 tablespoons margarine, the confectioners' sugar and 1/4 cup milk in a mixing bowl until smooth. Spread over the cake.

Yield: 12 servings

Pumpkin Roll

3 eggs
1 cup sugar
2/3 cup canned pumpkin
1 teaspoon lemon juice
3/4 cup flour
1 teaspoon baking powder
2 teaspoons cinnamon
1 teaspoon ginger
1/2 teaspoon nutmeg

1/2 teaspoon salt
Confectioners' sugar
3 ounces cream cheese, softened
1/4 cup (1/2 stick) margarine,
　softened
1 tablespoon mayonnaise
1/2 teaspoon vanilla extract
1 cup confectioners' sugar

Beat the eggs and sugar in a mixing bowl for 3 minutes. Add the pumpkin, lemon juice, flour, baking powder, cinnamon, ginger, nutmeg and salt. Beat until well mixed. Pour into a greased and floured 10×15-inch jelly roll pan.

Bake at 375 degrees for 15 minutes or until a wooden pick inserted in the center comes out clean. Remove to a wire rack and let cool 5 minutes. Sprinkle with confectioners' sugar. Invert the cake onto a clean dish towel. Roll the cake up gently in the towel from the short side. Let cool completely.

Beat the cream cheese, margarine, mayonnaise and vanilla in a bowl until light and fluffy. Beat in 1 cup confectioners' sugar until smooth. Unroll the cake and spread with the filling. Remove the towel and roll up the cake with the filling. Sprinkle with confectioners' sugar. Cover with plastic wrap and freeze until slightly firm. Slice and let warm to room temperature before serving.

Yield: 10 servings

Spiced Prune Cake

2 cups self-rising flour
2 cups sugar
1 cup vegetable oil
1 teaspoon cinnamon
1 teaspoon nutmeg

1 teaspoon cake spice
2 small jars baby food prunes
3 eggs
1 cup chopped nuts

Combine the flour, sugar, oil, cinnamon, nutmeg, cake spice, prunes, eggs and nuts in a large bowl. Stir until well mixed. Pour into a greased and floured 10-inch tube or bundt pan. Bake at 350 degrees for 55 to 60 minutes or until a wooden pick inserted in the center comes out clean. Remove to a wire rack to cool. If cake spice is not available, add an additional 1/2 teaspoon of cinnamon and 1/2 teaspoon of nutmeg.
Yield: 12 servings

Strawberry Cake

1 1/2 cups strawberries
1 package white cake mix
1 (3-ounce) box strawberry gelatin
3 tablespoons self-rising flour
1/4 cup water

1 cup vegetable oil
4 eggs
1/2 cup (1 stick) margarine
1 (1-pound) package confectioners'
   sugar

Slice 1 cup of the strawberries into a bowl and let stand until juice forms. Drain the juice and reserve. Mix the cake mix, gelatin and flour in a large bowl. Beat in the water, oil and drained strawberries. Beat in the eggs 1 at a time. Pour into 3 greased and floured 9-inch round cake pans. Bake at 350 degrees for 20 to 25 minutes or until the layers test done. Cool in the pans for 10 minutes. Invert onto a wire rack to cool completely. Sprinkle the strawberry juice on top of the cake layers. Mash the remaining 1/2 cup strawberries. Beat the margarine and confectioners' sugar in a mixing bowl until smooth. Beat in the mashed strawberries. Spread between the layers and over the top and side of the cake.
Yield: 8 servings

Turtle Cake

1 package German chocolate
   cake mix
1/2 cup vegetable oil
1/2 cup (1 stick) margarine,
   softened
1 cup water
3 eggs
1 (14-ounce) can sweetened
   condensed milk

1 (14-ounce) package caramels
3/4 cup chopped nuts
1/4 cup baking cocoa
1/2 cup (1 stick) margarine
1/3 cup milk
1 (1-pound) package confectioners'
   sugar
1/2 cup chopped nuts

Beat the cake mix, oil, 1/2 cup margarine, water, eggs and half the can of condensed milk in a bowl until well mixed. Pour half the batter into a greased and floured 9×13-inch baking pan. Bake at 325 degrees for 20 minutes.

Melt the caramels and remaining half can of condensed milk in a saucepan over low heat. Stir in 3/4 cup chopped nuts. Spread over the baked cake. Top with the remaining batter.

Bake at 325 degrees for 1 hour. Remove to a wire rack and let cool slightly. Combine the baking cocoa, 1/2 cup margarine and milk in a saucepan. Bring to a boil, stirring constantly. Pour over the confectioners' sugar in a bowl. Beat until smooth. Stir in 1/2 cup nuts. Spread over the warm cake.

Yield: 12 servings

Brownie Pie

3 egg whites
3/4 cup sugar
Dash of salt
1/2 teaspoon vanilla extract
3/4 cup chocolate ice box wafer
   cookie crumbs

1/2 cup chopped nuts
Sweetened whipped
   cream
1 tablespoon (or more)
   chocolate ice box
   wafer cookie crumbs

Beat the egg whites in a mixing bowl at high speed until foamy. Add the sugar and beat until stiff. Beat in the salt and vanilla. Fold in 3/4 cup cookie crumbs and chopped nuts. Spread in a 9-inch pie plate. Bake at 325 degrees for 35 minutes. Remove to a wire rack to cool completely. Spread with whipped cream and chill. Sprinkle with 1 tablespoon cookie crumbs before serving.

   Yield: 8 servings

Golf Digest ranked Greenville Country Club's Chanticleer course in the top one hundred courses in the United States.

Chocolate Pecan Pie

1 cup sugar
1/2 cup self-rising flour
2 eggs, beaten
1/2 cup (1 stick) butter, melted,
   cooled
1 cup chopped pecans

1 cup (6 ounces) semisweet
   chocolate chips
1 teaspoon vanilla extract
1 unbaked (9-inch) pie shell
Vanilla ice cream

   Mix the sugar and flour in a bowl. Stir in the eggs. Add the butter, pecans, chocolate chips and vanilla. Stir to mix well. Pour into the pie shell. Bake at 350 degrees for 30 minutes. Serve warm or chilled. Top with ice cream.

   Yield: 8 servings

Black Bottom Pie

14 chocolate cookies, crushed
5 tablespoons butter, melted
1 1/2 tablespoons cornstarch
1/2 cup sugar
4 egg yolks, beaten
2 cups scalded milk
1 1/2 ounces unsweetened chocolate
1 teaspoon vanilla extract
1 tablespoon unflavored gelatin
1/4 cup cold water
1 teaspoon rum
4 egg whites
1/2 teaspoon cream of tartar
Pinch of salt
1/2 cup sugar
2 cups whipping cream
1 tablespoon confectioners' sugar
Chopped pecans or chocolate curls
  for garnish

Mix the cookie crumbs and melted butter in a bowl. Press evenly into a 9-inch pie plate. Bake at 350 degrees for 10 minutes. Remove to a wire rack to cool.

Mix the cornstarch, 1/2 cup sugar and egg yolks in the top of a double boiler. Stir in the milk gradually. Cook over simmering water for 20 minutes, stirring often. Remove 1 cup of the custard to a bowl. Add the chocolate and vanilla to the bowl and stir until the chocolate is melted. Pour the chocolate mixture into the baked crust. Chill until set. Let remaining custard cool to room temperature. Dissolve the gelatin in the cold water in a small bowl. Stir into the custard. Stir in the rum.

Beat the egg whites, cream of tartar, salt and 1/2 cup sugar in a mixing bowl until soft peaks form. Fold into the custard. Spread over the chocolate layer in the pie plate. Chill until firm. Whip the cream and confectioners' sugar in a mixing bowl. Spread over the top of the pie. Garnish with chopped pecans or chocolate curls.

Yield: 10 servings

French Silk Pie

1/2 cup (1 stick) margarine
3/4 cup sugar
2 ounces unsweetened chocolate,
   melted, cooled
1 teaspoon vanilla extract

2 eggs
1 (9-inch) graham
   cracker pie shell or
   baked pie shell

Cream the margarine and sugar in a mixing bowl at medium speed until light and fluffy. Beat in the chocolate and vanilla. Add the eggs 1 at a time, beating for 3 minutes after each addition. Pour into the pie shell and chill, covered, for 4 to 24 hours.

Note: To avoid raw eggs that may carry salmonella, use an equivalent amount of egg substitute.

Yield: 8 servings

The Shriners Hospital for Crippled Children was established in Greenville in 1927. The hospital serves seven southeastern states and provides free care for orthopedically handicapped children.

Chocolate Chess Pie

1 1/2 cups sugar
2 heaping tablespoons baking cocoa
1 1/2 tablespoons flour
1/4 cup (1/2 stick) butter, melted

2 eggs
1/2 cup evaporated milk
1 teaspoon vanilla extract
1 unbaked (9-inch) pie shell

Mix the sugar, baking cocoa and flour in a bowl. Stir in the melted butter, eggs, evaporated milk and vanilla and mix well. Pour into the pie shell. Bake at 350 degrees for 30 to 40 minutes. Remove to a wire rack to cool.

Yield: 8 servings

Lemon Chess Pie

3 eggs
Grated zest of 1 lemon
1 cup sugar
1/4 cup milk

1 tablespoon butter, melted
1 tablespoon cornmeal
Juice of 1 lemon
1 unbaked (9-inch) pie shell

Beat the eggs in a mixing bowl until thick. Beat in the lemon zest and sugar. Beat in the milk, butter and cornmeal. Beat in the lemon juice gradually. Pour into the pie shell. Bake at 350 degrees for 40 minutes nor until firm; cool.
Yield: 8 servings

Ozark Pie

1 egg
2/3 cup sugar
2/3 cup self-rising flour
1 cup chopped peeled apple

1 teaspoon vanilla extract
1/2 cup chopped pecans
Vanilla ice cream or whipped cream
 (optional)

Beat the egg and sugar in a mixing bowl until blended. Beat in the flour. Stir in the apple, vanilla and pecans. Spread into a greased 9-inch pie plate. Bake at 350 degrees for 35 minutes or until golden brown; cool. Serve with ice cream.
Yield: 6 servings

Peanut Butter Pie

8 ounces cream cheese, softened
1 cup peanut butter
1 carton light whipped topping

1 1/2 cups confectioners' sugar
2 baked (9-inch) pie shells

Beat the cream cheese and peanut butter in a mixing bowl until smooth. Fold in the whipped topping. Stir in the confectioners' sugar. Pour into the pie shells. Cover and freeze for at least 8 hours before serving.
Yield: 2 pies

Fresh Peach Pie

8 ounces cream cheese, softened
1/4 cup sugar
2 baked (9-inch) pie shells
Sliced fresh peaches
1 cup water

1 cup sugar
1/4 cup cornstarch
1 (3-ounce) package peach gelatin
Whipped topping (optional)

Beat the cream cheese and 1/4 cup sugar in a mixing bowl until smooth. Spread in the bottom of the pie shells. Fill with sliced peaches. Combine the water, 1 cup sugar and cornstarch in a saucepan. Cook, stirring constantly, until thick. Add the gelatin and stir until dissolved. Pour over the peaches. Cover and chill for at least 4 hours or overnight. Top with whipped topping and serve.

Yield: 2 pies

Hawaiian Fruit Pie

1 1/4 cups sugar
1/2 cup self-rising flour
1 (20-ounce) can crushed pineapple
1 small package orange sugar-free
    gelatin

1 (21-ounce) can cherry pie filling
1 cup broken pecans
3 large ripe bananas, sliced
3 baked (9-inch) pie shells
Whipped topping

Combine the sugar and flour in a 3-quart saucepan. Add the pineapple. Cook, stirring constantly, until bubbly. Remove from the heat and stir in the gelatin. Add the cherry pie filling, pecans and bananas. Stir to mix well. Pour into the pie shells. Cover and chill until set. Serve with whipped topping.

Yield: 3 pies

Desserts

Charleston Benne Cookies

3/4 cup (1 1/2 sticks) butter,
  softened
1 1/2 cups packed dark brown sugar
1 egg

1 teaspoon vanilla extract
3/4 cup flour
1 teaspoon baking powder
1 cup benne seeds

Cream the butter and brown sugar in a mixing bowl. Stir in the egg and vanilla. Add the flour and baking powder and stir until well mixed. Form into 1-inch balls and flatten slightly. Spread the benne seeds in a shallow dish. Roll the balls of dough in the seeds. Place on a lightly greased cookie sheet. Bake at 350 degrees for 5 minutes or until very lightly browned. Remove to a wire rack to cool.

Yield: 2 dozen cookies

Favorite Gingersnaps

3/4 cup shortening
1 cup sugar
1/4 cup molasses
1 egg
2 cups sifted flour
1/4 teaspoon salt

2 teaspoons baking soda
1 teaspoon cinnamon
1 teaspoon ginger
1 teaspoon ground cloves
Sugar (optional)

Cream the shortening and 1 cup sugar in a mixing bowl. Add the molasses and egg and beat well. Sift the flour, salt, baking soda, cinnamon, ginger and cloves into a bowl. Add to the shortening mixture and mix well. Roll into small balls. Dip in sugar, if desired. Place 2 inches apart on a greased cookie sheet. Bake at 375 degrees for 10 to 12 minutes. Remove to a wire rack to cool.

Yield: 3 dozen cookies

Fudge Truffle Cookies

3 (4-ounce) bars German's sweet
   chocolate, chopped
2 tablespoons butter-flavored
   shortening
1 teaspoon instant coffee granules
3 eggs
1 1/4 cups sugar
1 teaspoon vanilla extract

1 cup chopped pecans
6 tablespoons flour
1 teaspoon cinnamon
1/2 teaspoon baking powder
1/4 teaspoon salt
Pecan halves (optional)
Confectioners' sugar
   (optional)

Heat the chocolate and shortening in a small saucepan over very low heat until the chocolate begins to melt, stirring constantly. Remove from the heat and add the coffee. Stir until smooth. Let cool to room temperature.

Beat the eggs and sugar in a mixing bowl at high speed for 3 to 4 minutes or until light and pale yellow. Beat in the chocolate mixture and the vanilla. Reduce the speed to low and beat in the chopped pecans, flour, cinnamon, baking powder and salt. Beat until well mixed. Drop teaspoonfuls of dough 2 inches apart on a cookie sheet coated with nonstick cooking spray. Top each with a pecan half.

Bake at 350 degrees for 8 to 10 minutes or just until set. Let cool on the cookie sheet for 1 to 2 minutes. Remove to a wire rack to cool completely. Sprinkle with confectioners' sugar when cool.

Yield: 4 to 5 dozen cookies

May this food restore our strength, giving new energy to tired limbs, new thoughts to weary minds. May this drink restore our souls, giving new vision to dry spirits, new warmth to cold hearts. And once refreshed, may we give new pleasure to You, who gives us all.

Spritz Cookies

1 cup (2 sticks) butter, softened
1 cup sugar
1 egg yolk
1 1/2 teaspoons vanilla extract

2 cups flour
1/2 teaspoon salt
Red and green colored sprinkles

Cream the butter, sugar, egg yolk and vanilla in a mixing bowl until light and fluffy. Beat in the flour and salt until well mixed. Place the dough in a cookie press fitted with a star tip. Press onto an ungreased cookie sheet. Top with the sprinkles. Bake at 350 degrees for 8 to 10 minutes. Remove the cookies to a wire rack to cool.

Yield: 4 to 5 dozen cookies

Wedding Cookies

1 cup (2 sticks) margarine
5 tablespoons confectioners' sugar
2 teaspoons vanilla extract

2 cups flour
1 1/2 cups chopped pecans
Confectioners' sugar

Cream the margarine, 5 tablespoons confectioners' sugar and vanilla in a bowl until light and fluffy. Stir in the flour and pecans and mix well. Shape into balls. Place on an ungreased cookie sheet. Bake at 325 degrees for 20 minutes or until lightly browned. Roll in confectioners' sugar while warm.

Yield: 5 dozen cookies

Nancy Reagan's Brownies

3 ounces semisweet chocolate
2 ounces unsweetened chocolate
1 1/2 cups (3 sticks) butter
6 eggs
2 cups sugar
2/3 cup cake flour

1 teaspoon baking powder
1 1/2 teaspoons salt
1 tablespoon vanilla extract
2 cups finely chopped pecans
Confectioners' sugar

Melt the semisweet chocolate, unsweetened chocolate and butter in the top of a double boiler over simmering water. Remove from the heat and let cool to room temperature. Beat the eggs and sugar in a mixing bowl until light and pale yellow. Stir in the chocolate mixture. Sift the cake flour, baking powder and salt into a bowl. Stir into the egg mixture. Add the vanilla and pecans and stir to mix. Pour into a buttered and floured 12×18-inch baking pan. Bake at 350 degrees for 30 to 35 minutes or until a wooden pick inserted in the center comes out clean. Remove to a wire rack to cool completely. Sprinkle with confectioners' sugar when cool. Cut into squares.

Yield: 4 to 5 dozen brownies

Chocolate Chip Squares

1/2 cup (1 stick) margarine,
    softened
1 (1-pound) package brown sugar
3 eggs

2 cups sifted self-rising flour
1 1/2 teaspoons vanilla extract
3/4 cup chopped pecans
3/4 cup chocolate chips

Cream the margarine and brown sugar in a mixing bowl until light and fluffy. Beat in the eggs, flour and vanilla. Fold in the pecans and chocolate chips. Spread in a greased 9×13-inch baking pan. Bake at 300 degrees for 45 minutes. Remove to a wire rack to cool. Cut into squares.

Yield: 2 to 3 dozen squares

Hello Dolly Bars

1/2 cup (1 stick) unsalted butter, melted
1 cup graham cracker crumbs

1 cup (6 ounces) chocolate chips
1 cup medium pecan pieces
1 cup sweetened condensed milk

Mix the melted butter and graham cracker crumbs in a bowl. Press into a 9×13-inch baking pan. Bake at 350 degrees for 10 minutes. Sprinkle the chocolate chips and pecans over the baked crust. Drizzle with the condensed milk. Bake for 15 to 20 minutes or until the chocolate melts and the top begins to brown. Remove to a wire rack to cool. Cut into bars when cool.

Yield: 3 dozen bars

Cranberry Caramel Bars

1 cup fresh cranberries
2 tablespoons sugar
2 cups flour
1/2 teaspoon baking soda
2 cups rolled oats
1/2 cup sugar
1/2 cup packed light brown sugar

1 cup (2 sticks) butter, melted
1 (10-ounce) package chopped dates
3/4 cup chopped pecans
1 (12-ounce) jar caramel ice cream topping
1/3 cup flour

Combine the cranberries and 2 tablespoons sugar in a bowl. Set aside. Mix 2 cups flour, the baking soda, oats, 1/2 cup sugar and brown sugar in a bowl. Add the melted butter and stir until crumbly. Remove 1 cup of this mixture and set aside. Press the remainder in the bottom of a lightly greased 9×13-inch baking dish. Bake at 350 degrees for 15 minutes. Sprinkle the dates, pecans and cranberry mixture over the baked crust. Mix the caramel topping and 1/3 cup flour in a bowl. Spoon over the cranberries. Sprinkle with 1 cup reserved oat mixture. Bake for 20 minutes or until lightly browned. Remove to a wire rack to cool. Cut into bars. These bars keep for up to 2 weeks in an airtight container.

Yield: 2 dozen bars

Lemon Squares

2 cups flour
1/2 cup confectioners' sugar
1 cup (2 sticks) unsalted butter
4 eggs
2 cups sugar

1/3 cup lemon juice
1/4 cup flour
1/2 teaspoon baking powder
1/4 teaspoon salt

Sift 2 cups flour and the confectioners' sugar into a bowl. Cut in the butter until crumbly. Press into a greased 9×13-inch baking pan. Bake at 350 degrees for 25 to 30 minutes or until lightly browned. Mix the eggs, sugar and lemon juice in a bowl. Sift 1/4 cup flour, the baking powder and salt into the bowl. Stir until well mixed. Pour over the baked crust. Bake for 25 to 30 minutes. Remove to a wire rack to cool. Cut into squares.

Yield: 2 to 3 dozen squares

Pecan Date Tarts

3 ounces cream cheese, softened
1 cup (2 sticks) butter, softened
1 cup flour
1 cup sugar
2 egg yolks

1 teaspoon vanilla extract
1 cup chopped dates
1 cup chopped pecans
2 egg whites
1/2 cup confectioners' sugar

Beat the cream cheese and 1/2 cup of the butter in a mixing bowl until smooth. Stir in the flour to make a stiff dough. Roll out the dough on a lightly floured work surface. Cut out 2 1/2-inch circles. Place each circle over the center of a cup in a mini-muffin pan. Press the dough into the bottom and up the sides. Cream remaining 1/2 cup butter and the sugar in a bowl. Stir in the egg yolks and vanilla. Stir in the dates and pecans. Beat the eggs whites in a mixing bowl until stiff. Fold into the filling mixture. Spoon into the pastry shells. Bake at 325 degrees for 25 minutes. Remove to a wire rack to cool. Remove the cooled tarts to a serving plate. Sprinkle with confectioners' sugar.

Yield: 4 dozen tarts

Chocolate Ginger Tassies

Pastry
6 tablespoons butter, softened
1/2 cup confectioners' sugar
1 egg yolk
1/2 teaspoon vanilla extract
1 1/3 cups flour

Filling
1/3 cup ginger or orange marmalade
4 ounces German's sweet chocolate
1/4 cup sugar
1/4 cup heavy cream
2 tablespoons unsalted butter
1/2 teaspoon vanilla extract

For the pastry, cream the butter and confectioners' sugar in a mixing bowl until light and fluffy. Beat in the egg yolk and vanilla. Add the flour 1/3 cup at a time, stirring well after each addition. Drop by teaspoonfuls into mini-muffin cups. Press into the bottom and halfway up the side of each cup. Bake at 350 degrees for 10 to 15 minutes or until lightly browned. Let cool in the pan for 5 minutes. Remove pastry shells to a wire rack and cool completely.

For the filling, spoon 1/2 teaspoon of ginger marmalade into the center of each baked shell. Melt the chocolate and sugar in the top of a double boiler over simmering water. Stir in the cream, butter and vanilla. Cook, stirring constantly, until the sugar is dissolved. Remove from the heat and let cool to lukewarm. Spoon 1 teaspoonful into each shell over the marmalade. Let cool completely. Store in an airtight container in a cool dry place.

Yield: 30 tassies

Bourbon Balls

1 (12-ounce) box vanilla wafers, crushed into fine crumbs
1 pound pecans, chopped

1 (10-ounce) package chopped dates
Good-quality Kentucky bourbon
Confectioners' sugar

Mix the wafer crumbs, pecans and dates in a bowl. Add the bourbon gradually and knead until smooth. Form into balls and roll in confectioners' sugar. Arrange the balls on a serving plate. Chill, covered, until ready to serve.

Yield: 4 to 6 dozen balls

Chocolate Truffles

2 cups (12 ounces) chocolate chips
1/2 cup (1 stick) unsalted butter,
   chopped into pieces
1 tablespoon vanilla extract

Baking cocoa
Sugar crystals or colored
   sprinkles

    Place the chocolate chips in a microwave-safe bowl. Microwave on High for 1 minute or until melted. Beat in the butter and vanilla until smooth. Chill for 1 hour or until firm enough to handle. Coat hands with baking cocoa and form rounded tablespoonfuls into balls. Roll in sugar crystals or colored sprinkles. Store in an airtight container and chill until ready to serve.

    Yield: 2 dozen truffles

Orange Coconut Balls

1 (12-ounce) box vanilla wafers,
   crushed into fine crumbs
1/2 cup (1 stick) margarine,
   softened
1 (1-pound) package confectioners'
   sugar

1 (6-ounce) can frozen orange juice
   concentrate, thawed
Flaked coconut

    Stir the wafer crumbs, margarine, confectioners' sugar and orange juice concentrate in a bowl until well mixed. Form into small balls and roll in coconut. Store in an airtight container for several days before serving.

    Yield: 3 to 4 dozen balls

Foolproof Campfire Fudge

32 marshmallows
1/4 cup water
2 1/2 cups sugar
1 (6-ounce) can evaporated milk
1/2 cup (1 stick) butter

1/4 teaspoon salt
1 1/2 cups semisweet chocolate
   chips
1 cup chopped nuts (optional)

Combine the marshmallows and water in the top of a double boiler over simmering water. Cook until the marshmallows are melted. Remove from the heat. Combine the sugar, evaporated milk, butter and salt in a large heavy saucepan. Bring to a boil over medium heat. Boil for 8 minutes, stirring constantly. Remove from the heat and add the marshmallow mixture and chocolate chips. Stir until the chocolate is melted. Mix in the nuts. Pour into an 8×12-inch buttered baking pan. Let cool before cutting into squares.

Yield: 4 dozen squares

Peanut Brittle

2 cups sugar
1 cup light corn syrup
3 cups raw unsalted peanuts

2 teaspoons baking soda
1/4 teaspoon salt

Cook the sugar and corn syrup in a heavy saucepan for 5 minutes. Stir in the peanuts. Cook to 300 to 310 degrees on a candy thermometer or until brittle when a small amount is dropped in cold water. Stir in the baking soda and salt. Pour immediately onto a buttered baking sheet with sides or 10×15-inch baking pan. Let cool until firm. Break into pieces.

Yield: 2 pounds brittle

Apple Crisp

4 cups sliced tart apples
   (about 4 apples)
2/3 cup packed brown sugar
1/2 cup flour
1/2 cup rolled oats

3/4 teaspoon cinnamon
3/4 teaspoon nutmeg
1/3 cup margarine, softened
Vanilla ice cream

Arrange the apple slices in a greased 8×8-inch square baking pan. Mix the brown sugar, flour, oats, cinnamon, nutmeg and margarine in a bowl until crumbly. Sprinkle over the apples. Bake at 375 degrees for 30 minutes or until the topping is golden brown. Remove to a wire rack to cool. Serve warm with vanilla ice cream.

Yield: 6 servings

Blueberry Crunch

3 cups fresh blueberries, or
   16 ounces frozen unsweetened
   blueberries, partially thawed
2 tablespoons lemon juice
2/3 cup packed brown sugar
1/2 cup flour

1/2 cup quick-cooking oats
1/3 cup margarine, softened
3/4 teaspoon cinnamon
1/4 teaspoon salt
Whipped topping or vanilla
   ice cream

Arrange the blueberries in a 9×9-inch baking dish coated with nonstick cooking spray. Sprinkle with the lemon juice. Mix the brown sugar, flour, oats, margarine, cinnamon and salt in a bowl until crumbly. Sprinkle over the blueberries. Bake at 375 degrees for 30 minutes. Remove to a wire rack to cool. Serve warm with whipped topping or vanilla ice cream.

Yield: 6 to 8 servings

Peach Crisp

4 cups sliced peaches
2 tablespoons water
2 tablespoons lemon juice
1 cup flour
1/2 cup sugar
1/2 cup packed brown sugar

1/2 teaspoon cinnamon
1/4 teaspoon nutmeg
1/2 cup (1 stick) margarine, melted
Whipped topping or vanilla ice
  cream

Arrange the peaches in a 9×9-inch baking dish. Mix the water and lemon juice in a small bowl and sprinkle over the peaches. Mix the flour, sugar, brown sugar, cinnamon, nutmeg and melted margarine in a bowl until crumbly. Sprinkle over the peaches. Bake covered at 350 degrees for 15 minutes. Uncover and bake for 30 minutes. Remove to a wire rack to cool. Serve warm with whipped topping or vanilla ice cream.

Yield: 6 to 8 servings

Fruit Dessert Pizza

1 (18-ounce) tube refrigerated
  sugar cookie dough
8 ounces cream cheese, softened
1/3 cup sugar
1/2 teaspoon vanilla extract

Sliced bananas, strawberries and
  other fresh fruit
1/2 cup orange marmalade
2 tablespoons water

Cut the cookie dough into 1/8-inch slices. Arrange the slices on a 14-inch pizza pan, overlapping slightly. Bake at 375 degrees for 12 minutes. Remove to a wire rack to cool. Mix the cream cheese, sugar and vanilla in a mixing bowl until well blended. Spread on the cooled crust. Arrange the fruit on top. Mix the orange marmalade and water in a small bowl. Glaze the fruit with the marmalade mixture. Chill. Cut into wedges to serve.

Yield: 10 to 12 servings

Charlotte Russe

1 envelope unflavored gelatin
1/2 cup cold water
4 egg yolks
1 cup sugar
1/4 cup sherry

4 egg whites
2 cups whipping cream
1 1/2 (3 1/2-ounce)
    packages ladyfingers

Sprinkle the gelatin over the cold water in a saucepan. Let stand for 1 minute. Cook over low heat until the gelatin dissolves. Remove from the heat and let cool slightly. Beat the egg yolks and sugar in a mixing bowl until thick and pale yellow. Stir in the sherry and gradually stir in the dissolved gelatin. Beat the egg whites in a mixing bowl until stiff. Fold into the egg yolk mixture. Whip the cream in a mixing bowl. Fold into the egg mixture. Line a 3-quart glass bowl with the ladyfingers. Spoon the filling into the bowl. Cover and chill.

Yield: 10 to 12 servings

Begun with a five-year public-private fundraising effort, The Peace Center for the Performing Arts opened in Greenville in 1990.

Chocolate F.E.A.S.T. Dessert

1 (9×13-inch) pan of baked
    brownies, cut into 1-inch squares
1 (6-ounce) package instant
    chocolate pudding, prepared
    according to package directions

1 (16-ounce) container frozen
    whipped topping, thawed
1 Heath or Butterfinger candy bar,
    crushed

Arrange 1/3 of the brownie squares in the bottom of a large serving bowl. Top with 1/3 of the pudding, 1/3 of the whipped topping and 1/3 of the crushed candy bar. Repeat 2 more times. Cover and chill for 2 hours.

Yield: 8 to 10 servings

White Chocolate Mousse

1 egg
1 egg yolk
6 ounces white chocolate, coarsely
    chopped
1 teaspoon unflavored gelatin

1 tablespoon light rum
1 tablespoon crème de cacao
1 cup whipping cream
Fresh mint sprigs and dark
    chocolate curls for garnish

Beat the egg and egg yolk in a mixing bowl until thick and pale yellow. Place the white chocolate in the top of a double boiler over barely simmering water. Cook, stirring constantly, until the chocolate melts. Stir 1/4 of the hot chocolate gradually into the egg mixture; stir the egg mixture into the hot chocolate. Pour into a large bowl and let cool.

Sprinkle the gelatin over the rum and crème de cacao in a small saucepan. Let stand for 1 minute. Cook over low heat, stirring constantly, until the gelatin dissolves. Beat the gelatin into the chocolate mixture a few drops at a time until smooth. Beat the whipping cream in a chilled mixing bowl at medium speed until soft peaks form.

Fold half the chocolate mixture gently into the whipped cream. Fold in the remaining chocolate mixture. Spoon into individual dessert dishes. Cover and chill for at least 3 hours. Garnish with mint sprigs and chocolate curls.

Yield: 4 generous or 6 small servings

Lemon Cheesecake

16 ounces cream cheese, softened
2 cups ricotta cheese
2 cups sour cream
1 1/2 cups sugar

1/4 cup cornstarch
2 tablespoons lemon extract
5 eggs, beaten

Beat the cream cheese and ricotta cheese in a mixing bowl for 5 minutes. Add the sour cream and beat for 5 minutes. Mix the sugar and cornstarch in a bowl. Add to the cheese mixture gradually, beating until blended. Beat in the lemon extract and eggs. Pour into a 2-inch-deep well-buttered springform pan. Bake at 350 degrees for 1 hour and 15 minutes. Turn off the oven and leave the cheesecake in the oven with the door closed for 1 hour. Cool in the pan on a wire rack. Serve at room temperature or chilled.

Yield: 10 servings

Pineapple Cheesecake

1/3 cup graham cracker crumbs
3 tablespoons sugar
3 tablespoons margarine, melted
40 ounces cream cheese, softened

1 1/2 cups sugar
3 eggs
1 (20-ounce) can crushed
   pineapple, drained

Mix the graham cracker crumbs, 3 tablespoons sugar and melted margarine in a bowl until crumbly. Press over the bottom of a springform pan. Bake at 350 degrees for 5 to 10 minutes. Remove to a wire rack to cool. Beat the cream cheese and 1 1/2 cups sugar in a mixing bowl. Beat in the eggs. Stir in the pineapple gently. Pour over the prepared crust. Place the springform pan in a baking pan. Add enough hot water to come 1/4 inch up the sides of the springform pan. Bake at 350 degrees for 65 minutes or until lightly browned. Cool in the pan on a wire rack. Chill, covered, until ready to serve. You may mix 1/4 cup ground pecans into the crust mixture before baking.

Yield: 15 servings

Flan

1/2 cup sugar
6 eggs
6 to 7 tablespoons sugar

3/4 teaspoon vanilla extract
3 cups scalded milk

Heat 1/2 cup sugar in a small saucepan over medium heat. Cook, stirring constantly, until the sugar becomes a golden syrup. Divide the syrup between 8 to 10 custard cups. Beat the eggs in a bowl. Stir in 6 to 7 tablespoons sugar and the vanilla. Add the scalded milk and stir well. Divide between the custard cups. Place the cups in a large baking pan. Pour hot water into the pan to come 1 inch up the sides of the cups. Bake at 350 degrees for 45 minutes. Remove the custards from the baking pan to a wire rack to cool. Cover and chill for up to 2 days. Serve chilled or at room temperature.

Yield: 8 to 10 servings

Lemon Custard

1 cup sugar
1/4 cup sifted flour
Dash of salt
2 tablespoons butter, melted
2 teaspoons grated lemon zest

5 tablespoons lemon juice
1 1/2 cups scalded milk
3 egg yolks, well beaten
3 egg whites

Combine the sugar, flour and salt in a bowl. Stir in the melted butter, lemon zest and lemon juice. Whisk the scalded milk into the egg yolks in a bowl. Add to the lemon mixture and stir well. Beat the egg whites in a mixing bowl until stiff. Fold into the custard. Pour into 8 greased 5-ounce custard cups. Place the cups in a baking pan. Pour hot water into the pan to come 1 inch up the sides of the cups. Bake at 325 degrees for 45 minutes. Remove the custards from the baking pan to a wire rack to cool.

Yield: 8 servings

Mouth-Watering Bread Pudding (Bill Cosby)

1/2 cup (1 stick) butter
2 cups half-and-half
1 cup heavy cream
1/2 cup honey
Dash of nutmeg
2 teaspoons vanilla extract

1 egg, beaten
6 to 7 slices dried bread,
   torn into bite-size
   pieces
Seedless grapes

   Combine the butter, half-and-half, heavy cream and honey in a saucepan. Heat slowly until warm. Stir in the nutmeg, vanilla and egg. Remove from the heat.
   Arrange half the bread pieces in a buttered baking dish. Top with a layer of grapes. Finish with the remaining bread. Pour the cream mixture evenly over the bread and grapes. Add a small amount of milk if any of the bread is not wet. Cover and place in a large baking pan. Pour hot water into the pan to come 1 inch up the sides of the baking dish.
   Bake at 450 degrees for 10 minutes. Reduce the heat to 350 degrees and bake for 35 to 40 minutes. Remove the baking dish to a wire rack to cool. Serve warm or chilled.
   Yield: 8 servings

 In 1938, Max Heller escaped Hitler's invasion of his native Austria by immigrating to the U.S. and he made his home in Greenville. Following a successful business career, Heller was elected to the Greenville city council in 1969 and served as mayor from 1971–1979. As mayor, Heller championed the revitalization of the downtown area.

Bread Pudding

1/2 cup sugar
1 cup evaporated milk
3 eggs, beaten
1 cup hot water
1/4 cup (1/2 stick) butter or
    margarine
1/4 cup raisins
1 teaspoon vanilla extract

1 apple, peeled, cored, finely
    chopped
2 to 3 slices dried white bread,
    torn in small pieces
2 to 3 slices dried raisin bread,
    torn in small pieces
Nutmeg

Mix the sugar, evaporated milk and eggs in a large bowl. Combine the hot water, butter and raisins in a bowl. Stir until the butter melts. Add to the egg mixture. Stir in the vanilla, apple and bread. Mix well. Pour into a buttered baking dish. Sprinkle with the nutmeg. Bake at 350 degrees for 45 minutes. Remove to a wire rack to cool.

Yield: 4 to 6 servings

Old South Banana Pudding

5 egg yolks
1 cup sugar
1/2 cup heavy cream
1 tablespoon vanilla extract

4 medium ripe bananas, sliced
1 (12-ounce) box vanilla wafers
5 egg whites
1/4 teaspoon salt

Combine the egg yolks, sugar and cream in the top of a double boiler over simmering water. Cook, stirring constantly, until the mixture coats a spoon. Stir in the vanilla and remove from the heat. Arrange the banana slices in a baking pan. Pour half the cream mixture evenly over the bananas. Top with the vanilla wafers and the remaining cream mixture. Beat the egg whites and salt in a mixing bowl until stiff. Spread on top of the pudding. Bake at 425 degrees for 5 minutes until the topping is lightly browned. Remove to a wire rack to cool.

Yield: 6 to 8 servings

Ice Cream Dessert

24 Oreo cookies, crushed
1/2 cup (1 stick) margarine, melted
1/2 gallon ice cream
1/4 cup (1/2 stick) margarine
1 1/2 ounces unsweetened chocolate

2/3 cup sugar
Dash of salt
2/3 cup evaporated milk
1 teaspoon vanilla extract

Mix the crushed cookies and 1/2 cup melted margarine in a bowl. Press into the bottom of a greased 9×13-inch baking pan. Freeze until hard. Thaw the ice cream until just softened. Spread evenly over the cookie layer. Refreeze. Melt 1/4 cup margarine and the chocolate in a saucepan. Stir in the sugar, salt and evaporated milk. Cook, stirring constantly, for 5 minutes. Stir in the vanilla. Remove from the heat and let cool for 5 minutes. Pour over the ice cream layer. Freeze until the chocolate is firm.

Yield: 10 servings

Butter Pecan Ice Cream

1/2 cup (1 stick) butter
2 cups broken pecans
1/4 cup sugar
3 cups light cream

1 cup heavy cream
1 1/2 cups sugar
1/4 teaspoon salt
2 teaspoons vanilla extract

Melt the butter in a medium skillet. Add the pecans. Sauté over medium-low heat for 5 to 6 minutes or until the pecans are lightly browned. Remove with a slotted spoon to paper towels. Dust with 1/4 cup sugar and let dry for 5 minutes. Combine the light cream, heavy cream, 1 1/2 cups sugar, salt and vanilla in an ice cream maker. Stir in the sugared pecans. Freeze according to the manufacturer's directions.

Yield: 1 1/2 quarts

Recipe Contributors

Lorraine Austell
Diane Bailey
Janet Bailey
Lula Bates
Teresa Betsill
Walter Betsill
Gloria Black
Louise Bodge
Evelyn Bond
Matthew Bostick
Marguerite Brace
Cheryl Bradshaw
Bev Bresette
Verena Bryson
Annette Burdette
Joe Burdette
Betsy Chambers
Calhoun Clark
Julie Clark
Meg Coffey
Karen Connor
Jane Decker
Judy Derrick
Carol Dobbins
Dick Dobbins
Linda Dzuris
Cynthia Eason
Kacky Elliott
Dorothy Ensor
Janet Ensor
Mona Ferguson
Tempie Fulmer
Judy Gange
Doris Gant
Bob Gardner
Mary Ann Gardner
Teresa Stewart Gardner
Rita Greiser
Gretchen Grounsell

Sally Hake
Dawn Halbert
Marlene Halbert
Beth Hamilton
Ginny Hampe
Marcia Harris
Maureen Harris
Nancy Harris
Philip Harris
Louise Heizer
Andrea Helm
Rt. Rev. Dorsey F.
    Henderson
Patsy Hill
Talle Hiltabidle
Dot Huff
Celia Jernigan
Ada Johnson
Dinah Johnson
Marie Kadow
Kathy Krasnoff
Helen Landmesser
Patti Lee
Marsha Lightsey
Wallace Lightsey
Noleen L'Insalata
Betty Lupo
Heather Mathewson
Marjorie McAlister
Pat McAlister
Susan McConnell
Robin Mill
Kat Mills
Kathy Moore
Lesley Moore
Howard Newton
Pegi Newton
Jean Olmsen
Hazel Pittendreigh

Kay Purser
Philip Purser
Lee Quinn
Frances Raikes
Lenora Rhodes
Waynne Roberts
Judy Rorick
Erna Samuel
Jenny Schofield
Lynn Schwarz
Elwanda Shugart
Kathy Shugart
Larry Shugart
Emily Neal Simkins
Jo Ann Smith
Jeanie Bouton Stuart
Gloria I. Suarez
Nanette Ternberg
Mary Vaughn
Gwen Vinson
Marilyn Weimert
Gloria West
Martha Whatley
Don Williams
June Williams
Candy Wilson
Cynthia Wilson
Johnie Woodfin
Amos Workman
Cecie Workman
Chart House
McCray Mansion Inn
The Palms Restaurant
Barbara Bush
Tim Conway
Bill Cosby
Katie Couric
Tony Danza
Nancy Reagan

154

Index

Let Us Keep the Feast
Food from the Foothills of South Carolina

Church of the Redeemer
Let Us Keep the Feast
120 Mauldin Road
Greenville, South Carolina 29605

Please send _____ copies of **Let Us Keep the Feast** at $19.95 each $ _____

Add postage and handling at $5.00 each $ _____

Total $ _____

_____
Name

_____
Address

_____
City   State   Zip

_____
Telephone   E-mail

Method of Payment: [   ] MasterCard   [   ] VISA

[   ] Check payable to Church of the Redeemer

_____
Account Number   Expiration Date

_____
Cardholder Name

_____
Signature

Photocopies will be accepted.